SOUTH ASIA

South Asia

A BACKGROUND BOOK

Angus Maude
M.P.

DUFOUR EDITIONS

CHESTER SPRINGS

PENNSYLVANIA

CONTENTS

MAPS

(drawn by Leo Vernon)

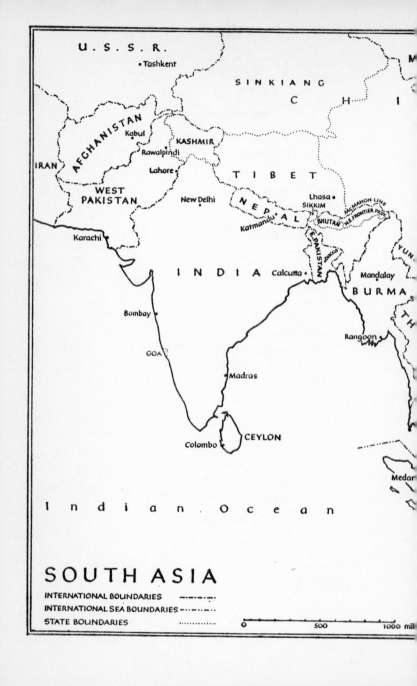

SOUTH ASIA

INTERNATIONAL BOUNDARIES	--·--·--
INTERNATIONAL SEA BOUNDARIES	--·--·--
STATE BOUNDARIES	·········

0   500   1000 mil

FOREWORD

THERE are so many experts on Asia at large today that it requires some courage to write another book about it—especially as all the experts review all the books.

Perhaps my main justification for taking the risk is that I have been able in the last fifteen years to look at South Asia from three quite distinct angles. As a British politician I have had to study and assess the political, economic and strategic implications, for the Commonwealth and for the Western alliance, of the post-war strife in Asia. As a newspaper editor in Australia I soon realised that the 'near North' was something very different from the 'far East'. In addition, I have visited nearly all the countries described in this book, from behind the Pathet Lao lines in Laos to the puppet President's office in Azad Kashmir; from Kabul to an Indonesian Army headquarters in the Celebes. The Asia revealed by these visits was something else again.

I have had the chance to talk to many of the leading figures of Asia who are mentioned in this book. To them, and to the countless Asians, Europeans and Australians who have helped me—politicians, officials, soldiers, dons, journalists and many others—I am deeply grateful. Too many people have helped me for it to be possible for me to name them—not that most of them would wish me to. Nor could I possibly list the whole range of written sources that have contributed to such knowledge as I have.

This book contains more historical background, and rather less comment and opinion in its treatment of individual countries, than is often found in books of this kind today. Perhaps the essence of most current problems in Asia can be better understood by studying how they arose than by much analysis of today's shifting scenes. In any case, they shift too fast for anything but a daily newspaper to keep right abreast of them.

Perhaps I should mention the nightmare problem of the transliteration of Asian names. I have tried to be consistent, and to use simple forms whenever possible without being obviously incorrect. Many of the names are difficult for English readers (and they are not made any easier by the fact that, for example, Diem is pronounced Zyem and Phoumi Poomy).

The experts will certainly catch me out in errors and inconsistencies. But perhaps I may be forgiven when it is realised that one is moving in a world where a Thai may write his King's name in English as Bhumibol Adulyadej, while a British expert spells it Phumiphon Adunyadet. I confess that this one upset me so much that I have cravenly not mentioned His Majesty at all.

ANGUS MAUDE

I

The Area Surveyed

'SOUTH-EAST ASIA' is always in the news. It is a term of almost infinite elasticity. The boundaries of the area are wherever you care to draw them. The most rigid definition would no doubt include only those territories lying between India, China and Australasia—namely Burma, Thailand, Indo-China, Malaysia, Indonesia and the Philippines.

This study has therefore extended the boundaries to include India, Pakistan, Ceylon and the states lying between India and China. This is South Asia. If there seems little logic in excluding Afghanistan, it will at least be found that this country is discussed in connection with the external problems of Pakistan and the possible future development of communist strategy in Asia.

This could, of course, easily have become a book about Asia, excluding the Middle Eastern countries and the Soviet Republics but including Japan, Korea, Mongolia and 'the two Chinas'. There are, however, reasons for omitting them other than that of space alone. While the area that has been chosen for study is in no sense homogeneous, the countries in it share a number of problems in common and present certain common problems to the West. It includes all the former colonial territories of Asia; it is the area in which the main ferment of Asian nationalism has been working; it has been the forum for the argument between the proponents of the doctrines of 'neutralism' and 'non-alignment' on the one hand and the allies of communism or the West on the other; finally, it represents the great no-man's-land of the Cold War, lying under the shadow of an openly revolutionary and expansionist China and the still enigmatic designs of Soviet Russia. It contains eight countries with frontiers bordering communist states.

This last fact has much more significance than is sometimes appreciated. It distinguishes South-east Asia sharply from those other 'under-developed' areas, Africa and Latin America. Obviously there are certain resemblances between these areas. All three are to some extent battlegrounds in the ideological struggle between communism and the West. All three belong, in global terms, to the 'poor south' rather than to the richer northern half of humanity. South-east Asia resembles Africa in being largely composed of newly independent colonial territories. But discussion of under-developed areas in general, of competition in economic aid, of the 'struggle for the minds of men', even the frequent use of the term 'Afro-Asian'—tends to blind people to the one really crucial difference between South-east Asia and the rest.

No single country in Africa or Latin America has a frontier with a communist state. And—with Cuba as the sole possible exception—no country in the world has come under communist domination since 1917 unless it was previously bordered by a communist neighbour. In South-east Asia communist infiltration across land frontiers—in Indo-China, in northern India, even perhaps in north Burma—is already in progress. If the process of attrition continues, the whole of southern Asia might one day be added to the communist bloc; and this would not be a victory gained by political ideologies or economic means, but a long, slow process of military conquest by the special techniques of infiltration and guerrilla warfare in mountains and jungle.

In this respect, then, South-east Asia more nearly resembles Europe than either Africa or Latin America. Because of these land frontiers with communist countries, the Cold War has a special intensity, with the perpetual threat of a shooting war added to it. It resembles Europe in two other respects as well. It has a long history of civilisation and of supra-national religions (to say nothing of international conflicts). And much of it was conquered and occupied by an Axis power during the Second World War.

*　　*　　*

South-east Asia contains a prodigious assortment of racial groups and sub-groups, their distribution appearing to bear little relation to present national boundaries. Indeed, some of the countries in the area have serious inter-racial problems within themselves. But the majority of the peoples of South-east Asia can be broadly divided into four main groups: the Mongoloid races which spread southwards from China; the Caucasians, or Aryans, who first entered India from the north-west and spread southwards and eastwards; the Dravidians, whom the Aryans displaced and drove southwards; and the Malaysians, who arrived in the area some 4,000 years ago and have only in comparatively recent years become numerous. There are also small minorities of aboriginal racial stocks—Negritos, Australoids, Melanesians and others—mostly living in mountains or deep jungle.

The history of the area has been one of continuous racial movement and conquest, the general tendency having been for northern races to spread farther and farther southwards. The Aryan conquerors carried the Hindu religion from the Hindu Kush to Indo-China and Malaysia. Buddhism spread southwards and eastwards from India, and later Islam swept into India with the sword and into Malaya and Indonesia with the voyages of Arab and Indian traders. Finally Christianity entered the region with the Catholic Portuguese and French, together with the Protestant English, Scots and Dutch.

South-east Asia has seen the rise and fall of many great territorial empires. The Khmers of Cambodia ruled in the twelfth century from the China Sea to the Indian Ocean. The Mongols penetrated at various times into India, Burma, Indo-China and even as far south as Java. The Thais once ruled in Siam, Burma and Indo-China. Early in the fifteenth century the Chinese sent naval expeditions throughout Asia, exacting tribute from Ceylon and Malaysia and reaching even to the Persian Gulf. India was almost united under the Buddhist Asoka, and 1,600 years later under the Mogul Akbar, before the British Raj was dreamed of.

Finally, in the early 1940s, Japan conquered the whole of

South-east Asia from the Indian frontier to the edge of Australasia.

*　　*　　*

When the Second World War ended with the traumatic shock of two atomic bombs dropped on the edge of Asia, the withdrawal of Japanese troops from occupied South-east Asia produced a vacuum which four distinct forces sought to fill. The European colonial powers returned to claim their former territories, for the most part unaware that the temporary Japanese triumph had fatally damaged Western prestige. Indigenous nationalist movements in these countries resumed their struggle for independence. Local communist parties, with varying degrees of encouragement from Moscow, set about promoting the Marxist-Leninist revolution. And the United States of America, with a genuine altruism as yet only hazily tinged with strategic implications, began to offer material and financial aid.

It is important to remember that each of these four forces was—and to some extent still is—separate and distinct. The nationalist revolutionary leaders were for the most part not communists—as so many Europeans have persisted in imagining. The Americans were far from supporting colonialism, despite the suspicions of many Asians. The history of Asia since 1945 has been the story of the interaction of four distinct forces, with the more recent addition of a fifth and complicating factor in the shape of a communist China with some emotional appeal to the Chinese overseas and intent on reviving ancient claims to suzerainty over her neighbours. To these has now been added a revived Japan, more or less in the Western camp and with increasing economic interests in South-east Asia.

From the moment the war ended, both Moscow and Washington found themselves in difficulties. The Asian nationalist leaders, intent on the anti-colonial struggle, looked with some suspicion on the communists who had supported the Allied (and therefore colonialist) cause since Russia entered the war.

14

Moreover, while the revolutionary surge in Asia was in part a social revolt against poverty and inequality, it was primarily a struggle for genuine independence and self-determination; there was no eagerness to substitute rule from Moscow for rule from London or the Hague. Nor did Stalin's dogmas permit him to see any future in supporting nationalist leaders who called themselves socialists but were not in fact communists. Meanwhile the Americans were beginning to suffer the first mild twinges of the schizophrenia that was bound to afflict a traditionally anti-colonialist people nearly all of whose allies were colonial powers.

Resorting to direct action, Stalin failed everywhere. The two regions in which Russian troops actually occupied Asian territory outside the Soviet borders in 1945 were Iran and North Korea. They do not lie within the area of this study, but the incidents are worth considering briefly because of their significance in the history of communist strategy in South-east Asia. In both places Stalin tried to pursue much the same tactics as in eastern Europe. He refused to withdraw his forces from Iran when British and American troops left in accordance with the Tehran Declaration. He then organised communist disturbances in the border province of Azerbaidjan and set up a communist puppet government there; he also supported a Kurdish autonomous régime in Mahabad. However, in the face of Anglo-American pressure in the United Nations, Stalin withdrew his troops from Iran in May, 1946 —perhaps under the impression that the country would later fall to communist subversion from within. The two puppet governments collapsed, and Iran is still an independent sovereign state.

The significance of this episode is twofold. First, it provides the only example of a communist withdrawal after the establishment of a régime backed by Soviet troops. Secondly, Stalin's withdrawal under pressure encouraged the Western allies to take a firm line in later crises, notably the Berlin blockade and the Korean invasion; even the dramatic confrontation of the 1962 Cuba crisis owed something to the lessons of Iran in 1946.

In Korea, where Soviet forces occupied the northern part of the country down to the 38th parallel, the United States were unable to extract from Stalin acceptable terms for carrying out the Cairo Conference agreement to unite this former part of the Japanese Empire under a freely elected government. A United Nations Commission, charged with the task of organising free elections in Korea, was refused admission to the Soviet zone. Elections were consequently held only in the American zone, and on August 15, 1948, the Republic of Korea under President Syngman Rhee came into existence south of the 38th parallel. To the north of the parallel a communist People's Republic was established, and recognised by the Soviet and its satellites as an autonomous territory. By the middle of 1949 both Russian and American troops had been withdrawn from Korea.

Meanwhile, the whole political and strategic picture of Asia was being dramatically redrawn by the emergence of a unified China under a strong communist régime. After eight years of war with Japan, the Kuomintang government was in no condition to cope with the rising power of the Chinese communists. With a record marred by rather more than the normal amount of cruelty and corruption, unable to attract the support of either peasants or intellectuals, Chiang Kai-shek could neither come to terms with the communists nor defeat them in the field. In 1949 Mao Tse-tung's forces occupied one province after another, and on October 1 the People's Republic of China was proclaimed in Peking. By the end of the year Chiang Kai-shek had withdrawn to Taiwan (Formosa), and Kuomintang power on the mainland was at an end, although garrisons were maintained on the offshore islands of Quemoy and Matsu.

The Russians, who had in the past collaborated for many years with Chiang Kai-shek, were as surprised as the Americans by the rapidity of his collapse. They had not supported Mao on anything like the scale of the Americans' support of

16

Chiang, and from the first Stalin found some difficulty in coming to terms with the new situation. The Chinese communists were in no mood to become his satellites. The Russians were outwardly cordial and reasonably generous with the material and technical aid needed to establish this new communist power as a going concern; but they had to recognise that a potential rival for the leadership of the Eastern bloc was now in the field.

The Americans suffered a traumatic shock from which their politicians and people have never recovered. Committed to the support of Chiang Kai-shek, they found the mainland of China not only closed to their trade and influence but controlled by militant communists. The results of the shock were far-reaching and unfortunate. Resentment and bewilderment provided the climate in which Senator McCarthy rose to the summit of his power; this in its turn made it politically impossible for either Democrats or Republicans openly to acknowledge the new facts of life in Asia. The ensuing policy of non-recognition of communist China, carried out with an apparently blind obstructiveness—together with the odium attaching to McCarthyism itself—made a most unhappy impression on the new Asian neutrals whom the United States were concerned to woo.

The Korean War completed the enormous shift in the power balance represented by the switch of China from the Western to the communist camp. When North Korean communist forces crossed the 38th parallel on June 25, 1950, to invade South Korea, the United States promptly led an armed intervention sponsored by the United Nations to repel them. The United Nations action against North Korean aggression soon became, however, a power struggle between America and communist China.

First, President Truman announced that Taiwan was to be 'neutralised', and that the U.S. Seventh Fleet would protect it against invasion from the mainland. Next, despite the unwillingness of the Asian neutrals in the United Nations, it was decided to pursue the North Korean forces beyond the 38th parallel. Faced with the possibility of the appearance of American troops on the Manchurian frontier, and no doubt also seeing an opportunity of bringing North Korea under Chinese control, Chou En-lai threw into the war Chinese forces on a scale sufficient to repel the United Nations armies. The war was reduced to a protracted stalemate, dragging on through dingdong fighting and lengthy truce negotiations till an armistice was signed in July, 1953. Korea remained partitioned at the 38th parallel.

Two points had been made. The first was that open communist aggression against a country in the Western camp would be met with armed force by the West. The second was that the new China was now a military power to be reckoned with on the mainland of Asia, and that the West—despite American fear and hatred of the régime—was not prepared to use nuclear weapons to attempt to destroy this power. Moreover, as events in Vietnam were to show in 1954 and in the 60s, the United States would in future be extremely unwilling to be committed to ground warfare against China.

One fateful result of the emergence of communist China was that the Americans were impressed with the need to secure Japan. It had already become obvious that the Japanese, who under American occupation had gone through a long and complicated process of demilitarisation and political and industrial reform, could be expected to agitate with increasing vigour for the return of sovereignty. The Americans were beginning to prepare the ground when the Korean war forced them to speed up the process. The Japanese base had to be secured by means other than occupation by U S troops which were badly needed elsewhere. A peace treaty made Japan independent; a National Police Reserve was set up for internal security, and the United States guaranteed Japan's external security in return for the use of military bases.

Thus Japan entered the Western camp. In it, with much initial American aid and the energy and technical skill of her people, she has made phenomenal progress. Neither sub-sequent Russian wooing and internal communist agitation, nor the attractions of neutralism to the former victims of the atomic bomb, has shifted her allegiance. Moreover, she has become an economic power in Asia.

Meanwhile Soviet Russia had been showing the same lack of skill in coming to terms with the newly independent colonial territories in Asia that it was later to display in the Congo and other African countries. Unable to introduce even guerrilla forces because of the lack of frontiers with communist countries, and compelled by dogma to regard the non-communist nationalist leaders as mere imperialist puppets, Stalin attempted internal subversion. Communist rebellions broke out in 1948 in Burma, Indonesia, the Philippines, Malaya and the Telengana district of Hyderabad (selected as a base for guerrilla operations designed to spread throughout India). In all these countries there were racial or religious minorities which, though themselves anti-communist, needed only the example of armed insurrection to take up arms themselves. All the communist risings failed—though none of them quickly—but rebel minorities have survived to this day in Burma, the Philippines and Indonesia.

Only in Indo-China were the communists able to make real progress. There, the anti-Japanese partisans had never been disarmed. In addition, French delays in coming to terms with the independence movement, and the confrontation of the playboy puppet Bao Dai with the tough, skilful, Moscow-trained Ho Chi Minh, gave the communists the chance to identify themselves with nationalist aspirations. War broke out against the French in 1946, and Ho Chi Minh was able to hold out until the arrival of a communist Chinese government on the northern frontier of Vietnam virtually ensured his success.

The negotiations at the Geneva Conference of 1954, which ended the Indo-China war and created the four new states of Laos, Cambodia and partitioned Vietnam, displayed to the world the Asian dilemma in which both America and Russia found themselves. By a quaint irony, the new conciliatory Russian line towards the Asian neutrals which followed the death of Stalin coincided with the adoption of something almost resembling a Stalinist line by the United States. Driven by his own religious anti-communist fervour and by political pressure at home, John Foster Dulles was castigating neutralism as 'immoral' and lecturing Nehru, U Nu, Sukarno and the rest on their 'duty' to toe the anti-communist line. Personally boycotting the Geneva Conference, Dulles refused to be a party to the cession even of northern Vietnam to communist control. The world was thus presented with the extraordinary spectacle of Molotov and Anthony Eden working in the closest harmony to achieve a settlement, each recognising that the other was seeking to restrain an ally willing to go to dangerous extremes. Britain and Russia between them averted a world war, but were left holding an embarrassing Indo-Chinese baby.

After Geneva, Dulles set about organising a collective defence system in South-east Asia. Of the five Colombo Conference powers, only Pakistan attended the Manila meeting that resulted in the formation of the South-east Asia Treaty Organisation (SEATO). India, Burma, Indonesia and Ceylon clung firmly to their policy of non-alignment. The Manila Treaty was signed by the United States, Britain, France, Australia, New Zealand, Pakistan, Thailand and the Philippines, and guaranteed its Asian members against aggression. The formula was carefully drawn to exclude Formosa and Hong Kong, but contained a protocol which stated that the signatories would invoke the Treaty if an armed attack were made on Laos, Cambodia or South Vietnam—even though those countries were not signatories.

The neutralist ex-colonial countries of Asia were, and still are, highly critical of SEATO. Most of them had troubles enough of their own, without wanting to be dragged into any more. India, which had fought a war with Pakistan over Kashmir, suspected that her neighbour had joined SEATO in order to secure Western military aid which could one day be turned against India. Burma and Indonesia were racked with rebellions, and were already showing signs of the chronic political instability from which only their armies have so far been able to rescue them.

In the following year, 1955, the Bandung Conference, which was sponsored by the five Colombo powers—including Pakistan—brought together 29 countries from Asia and Africa. This historic conference, representing 60 per cent of the population of the world, made clear the strength of neutralism in Asia. However, the triumph of the three Asian neutralist leaders—Nehru, U Nu of Burma and Sukarno of Indonesia—was slightly dimmed by the brilliant performance of Chou En-lai, who not only made a grand gesture for peace out of a tactical withdrawal from an awkward embroilment in Quemoy but succeeded in making several of the neutralists feel much more neutral against the West than they had been before.

The danger of Chinese expansion seemed to the non-aligned to be less than the risks of involvement in a cold war that might at any moment become not only hot but nuclear. Even India, China's rival for the leadership of Asia, appeared at that time to be watching the Chinese experiment with more curiosity than hostility; and a meekly pacific Chou En-lai at Bandung was more appealing than a militantly anti-neutralist Dulles plunging from brink to brink in Indo-China and Quemoy.

But this proved to be the peak of Chinese popularity. As Russia began more and more to woo the neutrals and ply them with carefully selective aid and credits, the face of China hardened. In 1957 Mao Tse-tung's 'Hundred Flowers' bloomed with such disconcerting vitality that they were sprayed with weed-killer within a month. In Tibet, occupied by the Chinese in 1950–51, an uprising in 1959 was crushed with a total ferocity amounting almost to genocide. Relations with India, now officially considered by Peking to be back-sliding into liberal capitalism, worsened from the middle of 1958, and China occupied large areas of disputed mountain territory on the Indian frontiers. There was a row with Indonesia over Sukarno's dispossession of Chinese traders. Only towards Burma and Pakistan did the face of China smile, which mightily increased Indian misgivings.

As Chinese self-confidence grew after the Bandung Conference, Peking began to assert with increasing vigour its own interpretation of Marxist-Leninist dogma. While post-Stalinist Russia talked of co-existence and Summit conferences—almost in terms of Nehru's Five Principles—China asserted the inevitability of an ultimate imperialist war against the advance of socialism. The Russians began to show signs of alarm, particularly at Chinese intransigence towards the neutral countries, in which the communist parties were being thrown into serious doctrinal disarray. Moscow withheld support from China in the Indian frontier dispute. An attempt was made to patch up the differences at the Moscow conference of 81 communist parties at the end of 1960; a compromise formula was arrived at, but the basic differences were unresolved—and indeed widened further in 1963. It remains to be seen whether Kosygin can close the gap.

* * *

Thus, over the whole South-east Asian scene, did the contending forces fill the vacuum left by the withdrawal of Japan. The colonial powers withdrew their sovereignty—Britain voluntarily, the French and Dutch perforce—but not their influence. The nationalist leaders brought their countries to independence, and began facing a troubled future greatly complicated by the manœuvring of the Cold War opponents. Communism made its bid for quick total victory in Asia and failed, but gained a substantial foothold. The United States sought to combine economic aid with the military containment of communism. In the mid-1960s Ho Chi Minh and Sukarno became neo-imperialists. Meanwhile the sleeping giant of China had awoken, a looming menace over South-east Asia, tough, confident and ineffably self-righteous.

2
India
═══════

IF South-east Asia is overshadowed by the looming menace of China, the future of the 470 million inhabitants of the Indian Union is one of the most momentous problems of the non-communist world. It has become almost a cliché to talk of the 'Indian and Chinese experiments', and to suggest that the future allegiance of Asia will be determined by the relative success of the communist régime in China and the democratic system in India. Like most clichés, it is dangerous.

To make India a kind of touchstone for the survival of non-communist forms of government in Asia is unfair to India and could be fatal for Asia. For one thing, it suggests that there will be a point in time—and at no great distance from the present—when it will be possible to strike a balance and say that the Indian or the Chinese 'experiment' has 'succeeded' or 'failed'. Once that assumption is made, it is obvious that in any competition thus defined India is severely handicapped. India is open to the world, with every failure and every shortcoming continuously under the microscopes of 'expert' foreign observers. What goes on in China is a matter of conjecture and controversy.

It is true that much of the conjecture about China is wild and hostile, and that she is the victim of much biased propaganda from Taiwan and the United States. But most of this has already defeated its own object and is discounted in Asia. Meanwhile, carefully selected visitors to China are shown carefully selected places and projects. Above all, it is possible for the Chinese Government to concentrate any chosen proportion of the national income on prestige projects to impress the world. The top of the iceberg is polished and decorated; the vast remainder is never seen. During the last few years it has been impossible for anyone outside China to do much more than guess at the extent of the food shortage there, or to prove whether or not a substantial proportion of the people in certain areas were starving. The extent of poverty and under-nourishment in India, however, is precisely observed and minutely documented.

In addition, China possesses one very great advantage which makes superficial comparisons with India dangerously misleading, since it is largely irrelevant to the efficiency of democratic institutions or totalitarian economic planning. It is simply that the Chinese—however often and deeply divided by civil wars—are a nation, and have been for many centuries. The Indians are not—yet. Brahman Hinduism gave India a kind of cultural unity that has endured, in much the same sense that Christendom built a European civilisation on Graeco-Roman foundations. The Congress freedom movement was based on a genuine national consciousness existing among a Western-educated cosmopolitan *élite*, but since independence was achieved the tendency has been for local nationalisms, based on linguistic regions, increasingly to preoccupy politicians to the detriment of Indian national solidarity. The task of creating an Indian nation is almost more important than the economic task—and may even be an essential prerequisite of success.

★ ★ ★

India is divided geographically into three main regions, and this division has largely dictated the course of its history. Indeed, it is almost true to say that there have been three Indian histories. The first is that of the largely Aryan north, in which the plains of the Ganges and the Indus have at various times been united in great empires ruled from Delhi. The second is the Deccan plateau, where Aryan and Dravidian stocks and influences merge, bounded by the Vindhya range on the north and the juncture of the Eastern and Western Ghats in the south. The third region is the Dravidian south, seat of the 'Three Kingdoms' of Tamilnad and birthplace of an ancient culture that may even be the oldest in India.

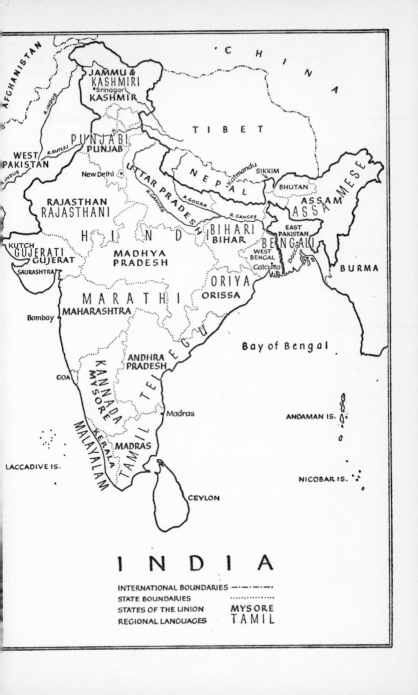

AFGHANISTAN

CHINA

JAMMU &
KASHMIRI
•Srinagar
KASHMIR

TIBET

WEST
PAKISTAN

PUNJABI
PUNJAB

R.SUTLEJ

R.INDUS

New Delhi

RAJASTHAN
RAJASTHANI

H I N D I

UTTAR PRADESH

R.GOGRA

NEPAL

Kathmandu

SIKKIM

BHUTAN

ASSAMESE
A S S A M

R.GANGES

R.GANGES

BIHARI
BIHAR

EAST
PAKISTAN

B E N G A L I

KUTCH
GUJERATI
GUJERAT

MADHYA
PRADESH

WEST
BENGAL

Calcutta

DACCA

SAURASHTRA

ORIYA
ORISSA

BURMA

M A R A T H I
MAHARASHTRA

Bombay

Bay of Bengal

GOA

KANNADA
MYSORE

ANDHRA
PRADESH

T E L E G U

KERALA

M A L A Y A L A M

T A M I L

Madras

MADRAS

ANDAMAN IS.

LACCADIVE IS.

NICOBAR IS.

CEYLON

I N D I A

INTERNATIONAL BOUNDARIES —·—·—·—
STATE BOUNDARIES   ················
STATES OF THE UNION   MYSORE
REGIONAL LANGUAGES   TAMIL

None of these regions has ever been wholly and permanently unified. Indeed, geographical and historical causes have led to an increasing distinctiveness of race and language. In the middle of the third century B.C., the great Maurya emperor Asoka—Nehru's favourite Indian hero—united north and central India under some sort of centralised political control and with the cultural links of the rapidly spreading Buddhist religion, but his empire did not long survive him. Six hundred years later the Gupta dynasty ruled a northern empire, but their writ did not run far into the Deccan. The Huns and other Central Asian invaders conquered, ruled, split and faded. The Deccan itself was temporarily unified by dynasties such as the Andhras and Chalukyas, while the Chola, Pandya and Pallava dynasties in the south were sometimes able to push their conquests into the Deccan.

At the end of the tenth century A.D. began the Muslim invasions which were to carry Islam the length and breadth of India. Muslim dynasties proliferated in the north, penetrated into the Deccan, destroyed the kingdoms of the south. Genghiz Khan made no headway against them, and even Tamerlane's conquest was short-lived; but in 1526 a descendant of both, the Mongol Baber, established the great Mogul dynasty in Delhi that was to last for 350 years.

By this time the main racial types and languages of the various regions of India were well established. Indo-Aryan, Dravidian and Mongoloid strains composed the racial types, while the languages developed as regional variants and mixtures of the Aryan, Dravidian and Tibeto-Burman tongues. Although the classical Sanskrit became more or less stabilised well before the Christian era and remained the literary language of Brahman Hindu culture, the original Aryan language had even earlier begun to evolve in different regional spoken forms, which later developed into the dialect groups of Hindi and Urdu, Gujarati, Rajasthani, Punjabi, Bengali, Assamese, Bihari, Marathi and Oriya (the last two being heavily influenced by Dravidian). Meanwhile, among the Dravidian group, Malayalam hived off from Tamil, and

26

Kannada and Telugu developed with strong Aryan elements. Each of these languages became the vehicle for a regional literature.

The Mogul empire reached its zenith in the reign of Akbar, during the second half of the sixteenth century, but it began to break up at the death of Aurungzeb in 1707. Nadir Shah of Persia plundered Delhi, and inside India the power of the Marathas and Sikhs was growing. Hyderabad, Oudh and the Carnatic became independent states, while Bengal, Bihar and Orissa achieved independence in all but name. This period greatly exacerbated the communal rivalries between Hindus and Muslims, which were to become so tragically important 200 years later. The Marathas, albeit with a roving eye for the main chance of conquest and plunder, purported to be fighting Islam (in the persons of the Moguls) on behalf of Brahman Hinduism. When their Hindu power grew too great, Islam struck back; a coalition of Muslim princes, led by Ahmed Shah of Afghanistan, broke the Marathas in 1761.

* * *

The break-up of the Mogul empire and the defeat of the Marathas, who had hoped to fall heirs to it, happened to coincide with the emergence of the British as the unchallenged European trading power in India. The Portuguese had long ago given up the struggle in favour of the Dutch; and, the Dutch having ejected the British from the East Indies, the British had driven the Dutch from the mainland of India. By the end of the seventeenth century the East India Company was established in Bombay, Madras and Calcutta, and was becoming not only a trading corporation but a military power in its own right.

The eighteenth century saw a desperate struggle by the French to oust the British, in the course of which both sides became intermittently involved in the regional and dynastic struggles of the Indian states. Clive having secured control of Bengal, Bihar and Orissa, Eyre Coote defeated the French and established British power in the Deccan. Despite attempts to restore their Indian fortunes during the Napoleonic Wars through alliances with local rulers against the British, the French were no longer serious contenders for power. From 1761 can be dated the beginnings of the British Raj.

* * *

British power was at first exercised solely in the trading interests of the East India Company, and in some areas under the form of acting on behalf of the nominal Mogul Emperor. Neither conquest nor political involvement was popular at home; successive Governors of Bengal and Governors-General—Clive, Warren Hastings, Wellesley, Minto, Lord Hastings and Dalhousie—were all attacked in England when they found themselves inevitably driven into further intervention and annexation in India.

The same story was monotonously repeated. Trade could not be 'secured' without territorial control, and as soon as one region was brought under control it seemed necessary to secure its frontiers by extending them. Modern India developed more or less haphazard.

There has been much discussion about the possible ways in which India would have developed without the British. It is not, on the whole, particularly profitable, but one or two points may be made. It seems fairly certain that the French would have conquered India if the British had not, and the subsequent histories of Indo-China and Algeria are relevant to the question of whether this would have been an improvement. If for the sake of argument, we omit the French as well, it would seem extremely doubtful whether anything could have stopped Russia from gaining control of Afghanistan, whose borders then extended well into Baluchistan. It is perhaps unlikely that Russia would have extended its control much beyond the Indus basin, but this is of course pure speculation.

The real controversy, futile as in many ways it is, is about what would have happened if no European country had attempted conquest in southern Asia. One may hazard a guess that the frontiers of Afghanistan would have extended beyond the Indus, and that Burma would have included not only Assam and Manipur but possibly East Bengal as well. What would have happened in the rest of the sub-continent? The Marathas insist to this day that they would ultimately have forged a united Hindu India. Indian nationalists, from Mr Nehru downwards, have consistently maintained that the physical absence of European rulers would not have prevented the spread of European ideas in India, that industrialisation would probably have proceeded faster but for British determination to sell British manufactures, and that modern methods of communication would ultimately have worked with the underlying unity of Hindu culture to produce a modern United India.

This may be so, but the argument takes a great deal for granted. Industrialisation, without an unacceptable degree of foreign economic control, demands a certain minimum of political stability and administrative efficiency, together with increasing productivity in agriculture. Indian agriculture is even now among the most primitive in the world, and it is hard to believe that such factors as the rigid feudalism of many regions, the rapacity of moneylenders and the virtual impossibility of proper stock management in the light of Hindu attitudes towards cattle would not have held back development even more in the absence of the British.

As to unification, it seems at least likely that Hindu-Muslim enmity would either have accelerated the total break-up of the Mogul empire without permitting any other race or dynasty to replace it or would have resulted in decades of destructive war. Further, it seems doubtful whether there would have been much inducement to improve linguistic communication outside the Hindi-speaking area of the north. It is no doubt true, as Indian nationalists have pointed out, that the imposition of English as the universal language of administration and higher education produced horizontal barriers between classes all over India; but without it, it seems almost certain that regional differences and distinctions would have been greatly and rapidly exaggerated.

* * *

It may be that future historians—including, perhaps, even Indian historians—will conclude that, while the British surrendered their control only just in time, the manner of their going enabled them to leave India in a better state than she could have achieved without them. But that is not to say that this state could not have been much better than it was. Not only could a greater degree of unity have been secured, but the rate of economic development and social reform could certainly have been much more rapid. It was no doubt a considerable achievement that the country was able to support such a vastly increased population at all (it increased in India and Pakistan from under 300 million at the beginning of the century to over 400 million at partition); but economic growth did little (if anything) more than keep pace with population growth, and the disparity of incomes between rich and poor was greater than anywhere else in the world. On balance, posterity will probably conclude that Britain should have developed India faster, both economically and politically, and perhaps conceded independence sooner. Nevertheless, the record is a good one by the standards of any other colonial power, and the subsequent history of India has paid some tribute to it.

* * *

The original purpose of the British in India was trade, and in the eighteenth and early nineteenth centuries many large fortunes were made there. In the great days of the East India Company, fortunes were also made by administrators, often as a result of services rendered to the dynastic and territorial ambitions of the Princes.

But the British Raj passed fairly soon beyond the phase of mere colonial exploitation and assumed, albeit reluctantly and never quite adequately, a responsibility for development and welfare. It is doubtful whether, for more than half a century before independence, India was on balance economically profitable to Britain. There were, of course, other considerations involved. India soon became, in addition to a source of cotton, jute and tea, a vast recruiting ground for mercenary soldiers. The Indian Army, though of somewhat uneven quality and perhaps never quite as good as the sentimental recollections of its proud and paternalistic British officers have suggested, was nevertheless a formidable force. On it the whole strategy of Commonwealth defence came to be founded, and it was this that really changed the balance of world power in 1947.

It was not until 1858, after the horror of the sepoys' mutiny of 1857, that control of the government and army of India was completely transferred from the East India Company to the Crown. Two systems of government continued, however, to co-exist. British India, which was administered directly by Crown officials responsible to the United Kingdom Government, comprised about three-fifths of the total area of the sub-continent. The remainder was made up of hundreds of 'Princely States', ranging in size from tiny feudal estates to great dominions such as Hyderabad, Mysore and Kashmir, which continued to be governed by their own rulers as tributaries of the British Crown and with the aid of British 'Residents'. The boundaries of the Princely States and of the Provinces of British India seldom owed their existence to anything more logical than the accidents of history.

The educational system which the British set up in India was from the first designed primarily to produce government officials and clerks. It owed much to the initiative of Lord Macaulay, who spent five busy years in India as a member of the Supreme Council. His famous Education Minute of 1835 proposed the deliberate creation of an *élite* that should be 'Indian in blood and colour, but English in taste, in opinion, in morals and in intellect'. To this end, as well as for administrative convenience in a country of diverse languages and dialects, the study of English bulked large in

31

the educational curriculum. Children began their education in the regional tongue, began to learn English at the secondary stage, and at the universities were taught and examined entirely in English.

The result was certainly the creation of an educated *élite* with a common language; but, convenient as the system was for the British, it had certain disadvantages for the Indians. In particular, it had an inhibiting effect on the development of Indian culture, since it tended to produce men who never became fully educated in any language at all. And it should not be forgotten that, before English was made the common language and the aim of higher education was degraded to the mere qualification of candidates for government employment, there had been a national Brahman culture based on an *élite* educated in the Sanskrit classics.

It was not to be expected that an English-educated *élite*, profoundly influenced by liberal, and later by socialist, political philosophies, would remain indefinitely quiescent under alien rule. Unnoticed by the rulers, a significant milestone in Indian history was passed in 1885, when the Indian National Congress was founded. Owing its inspiration to A. O. Hume, a distinguished British member of the Indian Civil Service, it was at first a moderate body which did no more than express mild aspirations towards a greater Indian share in government. In 1907 it defined its objective as the attainment by constitutional means of self-governing status for India within the British Empire. Congress being largely Hindu in its membership, it was joined in the field in 1906 by the All-Indian Muslim League.

Both these bodies threw up extremist elements, and Indian nationalism was in full ferment before the end of the First World War. Britain now began the process of gradualist reforms and concessions which never went far enough to satisfy nationalist ambitions and seemed, indeed, never quite to match in practice the fair words of promises for the future. The Montagu-Chelmsford Report led to the Government of India Act, 1919, which widened the franchise for the election of Indian members of Provincial and Central Legislative Councils and introduced—as a first step towards self-government—the principle of 'dyarchy' into the Provincial Governments. This transferred some branches of administration to Ministers who were responsible solely to the provincial Legislature, other portfolios being 'reserved' to Ministers responsible to the Governor and not accountable to the Legislature.

Some attempt to encourage the working out of common policies outside British India was made by the creation of a Chamber of Princes, although its function was purely deliberative. Meanwhile the Act gave a clear indication that the pace of progress towards independence was not intended by the British Government to be rapid; provision was made for the setting up of a statutory commission in ten years' time, to 'consider the possibility' of a 'further extension of responsible government'.

It was not to be expected that the Congress militants would be satisfied with this prospect, and there were many outbreaks of violence which were sternly suppressed. There would no doubt have been much more bloodshed than there was, had it not been that the leadership of Congress passed at this time to that legendary—and now, in India, canonised —figure Mahatma* M. K. Gandhi. It is as well to understand the significance of his achievements. He made of Congress a genuinely national movement, transcending not only regional and linguistic frontiers but the barriers of caste as well. This he did in two ways.

First, he provided an acceptable compromise between terrorist violence and ineffectual protest. His 'Satyagraha' campaign, with its non-violent civil disobedience, and the whole 'non-co-operation movement' attracted the support of moderate, peaceful, educated men who hated the thought of bloodshed; it provided an effective alternative to the methods

* 'Mahatma' (lit. 'great soul') is the most reverent of the honorific titles which it is the pleasant custom of Indians to bestow. Others are Pandit (learned), Sardar (leader), Acharya (scholar) and Master.

of the Bengali and Maratha terrorists, who would otherwise have captured the initiative in the nationalist movement.

Secondly, 'Gandhiji' made Congress a mass party by appealing directly to the peasants and low-caste workers and winning their allegiance and love. Before, the main aim of Congress had been to secure a greater share in government for the educated Indians who comprised the bulk of its membership: Gandhi made it an India-wide movement pledged to secure complete national independence.

In the early 1920s Gandhi gathered round him that band of Congress leaders who were the political mainspring of the independence movement—men whose election addresses or entries in *Who's Who* proudly proclaimed the number of times they had been imprisoned by the British. They included Pandit Jawaharlal Nehru, Sardar Vallabhbhai Patel, Chakravarti Rajagopalachari, Rajendra Prasad, Master Tara Singh, B. C. Roy, Acharya Vinobha Bhave, Morarji Desai, Jayaprakash Narayan and Acharya J. B. Kripalani. Despite their differences of race and temperament, despite disagreements about the tempo of their campaigns, about socialism or industrialisation, these men were united by their attachment to the Mahatma and by a passionate conviction that India could never be herself until she was governed by Indians.

But by which Indians?, asked the British. When, in accordance with the provisions of the 1919 Act, the Indian Statutory Commission was set up in 1927 and reported in 1930, the rationale of British gradualism was set out in detail. The Commission, of which the then Sir John Simon was chairman and Mr C. R. Attlee a member, provided in the first volume of its report a masterly descriptive analysis of India and its problems. The essence of the problem was summarised in the following extract:

> Down to thirty or forty years ago India stood entirely outside the influence of the course of political ideas which at length produced democratic self-government in some other parts of the world. But in the last generation she has been swayed, at one and the same time, by the force of several

34

conceptions which in Europe had followed a certain sequence. Thus, the struggle for power between rival religious communities, the rise of an intense national spirit, the spread of toleration, the growth of democracy, and the controversies of socialism, mark fairly well-defined epochs in European history. But, in India, these various influences are contending side by side for the allegiance of the politically-minded. The growth of national self-consciousness is retarded by communal separatism. The movement towards Western industrialism is countered by the return to the spinning-wheel. The equality of Asiatic and European is proclaimed, while the clash of Brahmin and non-Brahmin, or caste and outcast, is intensified. Ultra-democratic constitutions are propounded, although the long process which was a necessary antecedent to democracy in Europe, viz. the breaking down of class and communal and occupational barriers, has only just begun. Indian political thought finds it tempting to foreshorten history, and is unwilling to wait for the final stage of a prolonged evolution. It is impatient of the doctrine of gradualness.

It was, indeed. Everything the Commission said in this passage was no doubt true, but the winds of change were blowing ever more strongly. Thenceforth British proposals were continually overtaken by events. Congress virtually boycotted the Simon Commission and (apart from one visit by Gandhi to put its case) the Round Table Conferences that followed in London. During the five years that elapsed between the publication of the Report and the passing of the Government of India Act, 1935, Congress agitation increased and many of its leaders were imprisoned. The passing of the Act was marked in Britain by a bitter last-ditch opposition from the Conservative right wing, led by Winston Churchill. According to L. S. Amery—not the least imperialist of Conservative politicians—Churchill's speeches were 'purely negative and unconstructive', and his attitude towards Indian politicians 'consistently hostile and unsympathetic'.

What Churchill opposed was a comparatively modest advance, and one, indeed, which Congress rejected as totally inadequate. The new constitution, which came into effect in

35

1937, abolished dyarchy in the Provinces and gave them substantial autonomy, subject to certain reserved 'safeguards'; a measure of dyarchy was introduced at the centre, and provision was made for the unification of India in a federation when a sufficient number of Princely States was willing to accede. Both Congress and the Muslim League repudiated the federal scheme, but they contested the Provincial elections. Congress won power in seven Provinces and, after an initial refusal to operate the constitution, formed governments. Relations between Congress and the Muslim League went from bad to worse. At the same time, the radicalism of Congress governments in the Provinces frightened the Princes away from the idea of federation.

Congress objected bitterly to the proclamation of India's entry into the Second World War, and in November, 1939, all Congress Provincial Governments resigned, their powers being taken over by the Governors. In March, 1942, Sir Stafford Cripps went to India to attempt to negotiate an agreement with Congress leaders for their support in the war effort—now all the more vital because of the Japanese victories which were bringing Japan closer to the Indian frontier with Burma—on the basis of a promise of 'Dominion Status' after the war. It was scarcely to be expected that Congress leaders would be much attracted by a vague promise, without precise undertakings and dates, from a British Government of which Churchill was the head, and the Cripps mission failed.

A few months afterwards Congress passed the famous 'Quit India' resolution, demanding immediate independence. The Indian Government promptly arrested its leaders (including Nehru) and imprisoned them. There were many riots and acts of sabotage, and some extreme nationalists, led by Subhas Chandra Bose, formed (outside the country) a Provisional Government of Free India, which co-operated with the Japanese and ultimately contributed a contingent to their abortive invasion of Assam.

*   *   *

The end of the war more or less coincided with the election of a Labour Government in Britain and of large Provincial majorities for Congress and the Muslim League in the Hindu and Muslim constituencies respectively. The stage was set for the granting of independence. So far, however, from the final arguments being between Indians and British over the terms and timing of the transfer of power, the controversy resolved itself into one between the Congress Hindus and the Muslim League. Ever since 1940 the League had been asserting, with increasing force, that the Muslims were not merely a minority community in India but a separate nation, that the sub-continent must be partitioned and an independent Muslim state of Pakistan set up to embrace the Muslim majority areas.

This fundamental division between the Hindu and Muslim communities proved fatally deeper than the racial and linguistic differences of India. The tragedy of partition has inclined some of India's sympathisers to harsh criticism of the Muslims for what they regard as mere religious bigotry. It is not, however, as simple as that. (Even if it were, British critics might do well to remember the Simon Commission's warning against expecting in India a degree of tolerance and sophistication which it took Europe many centuries to achieve—and which has perhaps not yet been wholly achieved in Ireland, for example.)

There are two large considerations to be borne in mind. The first is that Islam is a supra-national religion, which Brahman Hinduism today is not. It is not only that the two religions involve profound differences in tradition, social customs and even personal character; many Muslims do deeply feel the need, if not for a theocratic state, at least for a form of government based on the ideals and customs of Islam—and for a government, moreover, which will stand in a special relationship with other Muslim states abroad.

Secondly the Indian Muslims had some reason to fear permanent subjection—even with constitutional safeguards for Muslim states in an Indian federation—to an overwhelming Hindu majority. The Muslims had to a considerable extent ruled India before the advent of the British, but it was the adaptable Hindus who chiefly embraced English education and came to the top in politics, administration, and above all in the industry and commerce of British India. So long as the British ruled almost autocratically in the Provinces and Muslim Princes retained control of their states, this did not matter too much, for the rights of Muslim minorities were in the last resort protected. But if the whole of India were to be ruled by Indian governments elected by universal suffrage, there would be no guarantee that the economic dominance of the Hindus would not be accentuated and that the majority would not seek to control or abolish the customs and distinctive features of Islam.

A British Cabinet Mission visited India in March, 1946, and entered into long discussions with Gandhi and Nehru, and with Mohammed Ali Jinnah, President of the Muslim League. There were disagreements between Hindus and Muslims over the proposed federal constitution, but still more over the proposals for an interim government. The talks broke down, and Jinnah committed the Muslims finally and irrevocably to Pakistan. In August communal riots broke out, with appalling bloodshed. In February, 1947, the British Government fixed a time-limit and announced that it would transfer power willy-nilly. Largely thanks to the diplomacy of the new Viceroy, Lord Mountbatten—who had, in the closing stages of the war against Japan, shown perception and moderation in his handling of South-east Asian affairs— agreement on partition was reached. At midnight on August 14, 1947, the two sovereign independent Commonwealth states of India and Pakistan came into existence.

* * *

The partition of British India involved a most awkward division of territory which had almost nothing to recommend it except that it appeared to do less violence to religious and communal sentiment than any alternative division would have

38

done. On geographical, economic, political and strategic grounds there was little to be said for it. It involved not only the partition of the sub-continent into two countries, but the division of Pakistan into two separate halves and the splitting between India and Pakistan of the two former Provinces of Bengal and the Punjab.

In both of these Provinces substantial minorities of Hindus were left in Pakistan and of Muslims in India. This led almost immediately to communal strife, resulting in appalling massacres and mass flights of refugees across both frontiers. Even now there are still substantial minorities in both India and Pakistan, but religious disorders are not now common except when the Kashmir issue inflames partisans.

The next major problem of partition was the future of the 562 Princely States—two-fifths of the whole area of the sub-continent. At the granting of independence to the two successor countries, the paramountcy of the British Crown over the States lapsed, together with all the treaties and agreements with them. The Viceroy had advised all the Princes to accede to one or other of the new countries, and nearly all of them did so. In the end, 554 out of the 562 States acceded to India; some 140 of the larger ones, which had retained internal autonomy under the British, acceded only in respect of such matters as defence, foreign relations and communications—in other words, the matters which had previously been reserved to the British Raj. There were, however, three significant exceptions. Two of these, Hyderabad and the State of Jammu and Kashmir, were the largest States in the sub-continent; the third, Junagadh, was a small enclave in the Kathiawar Peninsula. Junagadh, which had a Muslim ruler and a predominantly Hindu population, acceded to Pakistan, although it was entirely enclosed by India and was some 200 miles from the frontier of West Pakistan. The Government of India took a somewhat high line about this, and incorporated the State into India by force. There is no doubt that this was the tidiest solution, although it did not perhaps provide the happiest precedent for India's subsequent constitutional arguments about Kashmir.

The Nizam of Hyderabad, another Muslim ruler with a largely Hindu population, wished to remain independent. This, under the Act, he was entitled to do. However, his feudal rule was not entirely popular, and in 1948 there was a communist rising in the Telengana district and much unrest throughout the State. After a long dispute with the Nizam, the Indian Government carried out what it described as a 'police action'. In other words, it annexed the State by force. As with Junagadh, it can certainly be argued that Hyderabad could not indefinitely have remained as an enclave in India; nevertheless, it was becoming clear that the spiritual heirs of Gandhi would not shrink from using force against those who stood in their way—such as the Portuguese in Goa.

The third, and by far the most difficult, case was that of the State of Jammu and Kashmir. This was a predominantly Muslim State, but with a Hindu ruler. What made it a critical area was that it lay on the frontiers of both India and Pakistan, and was in addition of some strategic importance, since it also bordered on Tibet and China and included the regions of Gilgit and Ladakh to which the Chinese have laid claim. It may be said that geographically it would seem perhaps rather to belong with Pakistan than with India, since its rivers and its trade flowed mainly towards Pakistan. Moreover, its inhabitants were mainly Muslim. It is not, however, surprising that the Hindu ruler should have felt that his own personal position would be seriously weakened if his State were incorporated in a Muslim country. Although he hoped to retain some measure of independence, he nevertheless recognised the natural orientation of Kashmir towards Pakistan by concluding a 'standstill agreement' with it. This was an arrangement that was common at the outset of partition, under which one of the two successor states to the British Raj undertook temporarily to run the communication and other services which had previously been managed by the central government for the Princely States. It was small wonder, then, that the Pakistanis should have confidently expected that, if and when the Maharajah decided to accede to one country or another, it would be to Pakistan.

So, in all probability, he would have done in the end if matters had been allowed to take their course peacefully. But the situation in Kashmir became more and more difficult as the infection of communal disorders spread from the Punjab. The ruling family had never been particularly popular with their Muslim subjects, and these now began to demonstrate in favour of immediate accession to Pakistan. Unfortunately, at this stage large numbers of tribesmen from the North West Frontier Province (which had become part of Pakistan) began to stream into Kashmir, in the words of one writer 'fired by prospects of a holy war and loot'. It is doubtful whether this incursion was deliberately encouraged, let alone organised, by the Government of Pakistan in the first instance; but the tribesmen certainly came from territory which was at least nominally under its control, and it made no apparent move to check them.

The Maharajah then appealed to the Indian Government for help and protection, but this was refused unless he signified the accession of Jammu and Kashmir to India. This he did, with the inevitable result that Muslim agitation was intensified. When Indian troops began to gain the upper hand, Pakistan started to aid the tribesmen and the Kashmir rebels, finally entering the field with regular Pakistani forces. India and Pakistan were now at war, and remained so for about a year, when the UN arranged a cease-fire which left the State partitioned. The bitterness arising out of this dispute, in which both sides were convinced of the absolute validity of their moral and legal rights, was a historic disaster. It also provided an example—of which the conquest of Goa in 1962 was another—of Indian ruthlessness in defence of what Indians believe to be their rights and needs. A further case has been the bitter war lasting more than 12 years against the Naga hillmen seeking independence on the north-east border.

Even so, most observers were surprised when, after some

Pakistani military activity on the Kashmir cease-fire line, India invaded Pakistan on September 6, 1965. The second Indo-Pakistan war ended in military stalemate and another cease-fire.

* * *

The new Dominion of India lasted, in its transitional form, for $2\frac{1}{2}$ years. On January 26, 1950, the present constitution came into force, and the Union of India emerged as a republic, within the Commonwealth and acknowledging the King of the United Kingdom as Head of the Commonwealth. The constitution was that of a Union of States, with a division of powers between Union and State legislatures; the central government consisted of an elected President and two elected Houses of Parliament, the Rajya Sabha (Upper House) and Lok Sabha (Lower House).

In 1952 the first general elections were held under the new constitution, on a basis of universal adult suffrage. The Congress Party, still secure in its position of successful architect of independence—and freed from the opposition of the Muslim League—won 75 per cent of the seats in the Lok Sabha, a triumph which was repeated in 1957. In between these two elections the political map of India was redrawn, and the tremendously important principle of linguistic states was introduced. Certainly some rationalisation was needed, for the old boundaries of the British Provinces and Princely States seldom bore any relation to geography or logic, and the situation had not been much improved by the regrouping of the Princely States when they had been completely integrated into the Union (as, by the end of 1949, all of them except Jammu and Kashmir had been, the rulers agreeing to abdicate their rule in exchange for generous government pensions for life). In particular, the State boundaries bore little relation to racial and language groupings.

The first move was the construction in 1953 of the new State of Andhra out of the Telegu-speaking areas of Madras. Apart from Bihar and the old Hindi-speaking United Provinces of Agra and Oudh (renamed Uttar Pradesh, to preserve the familiar initials UP), none of the old Provinces or States remained in recognisable form. Hyderabad disappeared, Mysore was extended to include the whole Kannada-speaking region, Madras was made co-extensive with the old Tamilnad and Kerala with the Malayalam-speaking area. Rajasthan, Orissa, the Punjab, Assam and West Bengal became States in which their own native language predominated. The old Central Provinces were expanded into the vast State of Madhya Pradesh. Finally, in 1960, the great State of Bombay was split—after much controversy—into the two linguistic States of Maharashtra and Gujerat.

*   *   *

So the pattern of the new India was set. The Indian nationalism that Gandhi, Nehru and Patel had awoken to carry the Congress through the struggle for independence had achieved its first great objective. It remained to be seen whether this unifying force was strong enough, without the challenge of a common 'enemy', to secure the even more important goal of welding India into a nation.

In the years after 1947 it seemed as though the underlying unity of India which the struggle for independence had evoked—that communal self-consciousness which, in confrontation with the British, made Bengali, Maratha, Punjabi and Tamil all feel themselves to be 'Indians', although they could perhaps only communicate with each other in the English language—was being systematically weakened by the violent surge of regional linguistic self-consciousness. So much so that many anxious and perceptive observers began to fear that centrifugal tendencies would ultimately destroy the Union, or at best that the Union could only be held together by a totalitarian régime differing widely from the democratic ideas of Pandit Nehru and the authors of the constitution.

India's friends must hope that this view is too gloomy, although it would be foolish to deny that the dangers exist.

There is no doubt that the regional 'nationalisms' of India have given rise to many destructive rivalries and have drawn off from the centre much political talent and energy. In Andhra, Kerala and other regions the Communist Party has been able to exploit and profit by linguistic and caste rivalries. But it is surely not surprising, and not entirely undesirable, that regional patriotism and local cultures should have undergone this great resurgence. They have, after all, long traditions behind them, and they were undoubtedly held back by the centralising tendencies of the British and the English-oriented education they imposed. With independence they were themselves liberated.

This diversity of language, and the obvious intention of the regional communities to foster the development of the local tongues, underlines the need for a linking language which will not only serve as a means of communication and facilitate central government but will also signify and enhance nationhood. At present, the business of Parliament and of central administration is carried on in English, which most educated Indians still speak; but the constitution stated that the official language was to be Hindi (in the Devanagari script), and in 1955 the Ministry of Education laid down a programme for the progressive replacement of English by Hindi over a period of 15 years. It is, obviously, only natural that independent Indians should wish to have a linking language that is Indian; but the difficulties involved are very great. For one thing, neither Hindi nor most of the regional languages have yet evolved into adequate vehicles for modern needs: they have very limited technical vocabularies and often lack clarity and precision in the contexts of today. They will, of course, develop to meet the needs, but in the meantime the educational problems involved are considerable. The regional universities are still having trouble over textbooks.

The real danger is that India may, at least for an interim period, be left with no widely known linking language at all. There is considerable resistance to the use of Hindi in some states—particularly Tamilnad—and meanwhile the teaching of English is perceptibly on the decline. Hindi, in one form or another, is certainly the language spoken by more people than any other: but, even if one includes in the Hindi 'bloc' Rajasthani, Bihari, Punjabi and Urdu (although the Punjabi Sikhs and the Muslim speakers of Urdu use distinct scripts), it still totals well under half the population of India. There are eight other major language groups.

Nor is there complete agreement as to what form of 'Hindi' the national linking language should be. The official purists envisage a university-taught form of the near-Sanskrit literary Hindi, but the objection to this is simply that almost nobody speaks it. It may be that in the end a form of Hindustani will emerge that will be adequate for most purposes and generally comprehensible. Meanwhile, particularly in Tamilnad, the language issue has caused great dissension. In February, 1965, Mr Shastri, then Prime Minister, promised to suspend the enforcement of Hindi as the official tongue.

The need for such a bond of union is obvious, quite apart from the practical difficulties which the lack of a widely known, acceptable and efficient linking language would involve. Even if the language problem is solved, there are still those who fear that the Union may not hold together. It is not only that regional rivalries and preoccupation with local affairs may encourage separatism. There is also the possibility that the Congress Party might begin to split up after the death of Mr Nehru in 1964.

The Congress Party has been able to retain its virtual monopoly of central government ever since independence, and is still overwhelmingly dominant in the states. Such opposition parties as there are have all failed to secure significant support among the mass of the electorate, which has voted almost automatically for Congress as the party of independence and of Mr Nehru. Moreover, even these small parties are largely splinter groups from Congress itself. They include the Praja Socialist Party, which broke away under the leadership of the former resistance hero Jayaprakash Narayan and was later led by the intellectual Asoka Mehta;

the Jan Sangh, a theocratic Hindu nationalist party; and the right-wing Swatantra Party, formed in 1959 by the veteran Congress leader Chakravarti Rajagopalachari, a former Prime Minister of Madras and later the first Indian Governor General.

Yet none of these parties succeeded in making any effective challenge to Congress in the 1962 elections. Even the communists did better; but they, although they have had their regional successes (generally by cashing in on communal or linguistic conflicts) and even succeeded in forming a short-lived Government in Kerala in 1957, are rent by divisions and have naturally lost even more ground since the Chinese invasions.

Perhaps one reason for the absence of effective opposition parties in India (except for a few which, as in Tamilnad, represent minority separatist movements) is that the Congress Party itself, having started as an independence movement embracing a wide variety of shades of opinion, is still something of a coalition within which most of the political spectrum is visible, from conservative to left-wing socialist.

It was often argued, before the death of Pandit Nehru, that this heterogeneity would make it all the more likely that Congress would break up when he was gone. Until the fall of V. K. Krishna Menon, perhaps Nehru's closest confidant, it was widely supposed that the Congress left wing—and even perhaps some of the communists—would rally to Menon, precipitating a break with the right and centre, which had no love for him. He appeared, however, to have been pretty thoroughly discredited by the apparent failure of his efforts as Minister of Defence before and after the Chinese invasion of 1962. Although he won his Bombay constituency handsomely in a much-publicised fight against the former Congress leader Acharya J. B. Kripalani, Menon was soon dropped from his job.

In 1963 Congress was becoming worried about the faction fights within it and the state of its organisation. The so-called 'Kamaraj plan', produced by the Madras Congress leader

Kamaraj Nadar, called for the resignation of a number of Union and State ministers and their diversion to party work among the people. Resignations (not very voluntary) there were, but the wrangles over succession probably inflicted more wounds than the plan's benefits justified.

When Nehru died in 1964, Congress did not split. There was, however, enough conflict over the succession to make it necessary to elect a compromise candidate as leader. The left would not have the moderate Morarji Desai, for many years Finance Minister under Nehru, while the right would not have Nehru's daughter Mrs Indira Gandhi. In the end the compromise choice fell on a modest little man named Lal Bahadur Shastri. Mr Shastri struggled as best he could with an awkward legacy, but he had neither charisma nor dynamism, and no one knew how long he would last.

In the event, Mr Shastri succeeded better than had been expected. An inner core of toughness enabled him to enforce compromises on rival colleagues and interests. Indeed, his militancy during the Indo-Pakistan war of 1965 made him a national hero, and his death at the Tashkent conference in January, 1966, was deeply mourned.

This time the succession fell on Mrs Indira Gandhi. She inherited a daunting task: the aftermath of the Pakistan war, desperate economic difficulties, and a growing threat of famine despite Western grain shipments.

*　　*　　*

One of the obvious dangers to Congress unity—as to the unity of India itself—is the tension between the largely Aryan and Hindi-speaking north and the predominantly Dravidian south. So far from this historic cleavage having been healed since independence, there are signs that it has increased and may be still increasing.

One effect of this rivalry, and indeed of the rivalries between all the linguistic states, is to complicate the already enormous problems of India's economic development. Central government finance and investment have often to be allocated in directions which are by no means the most obviously beneficial to the national interests but which are demanded by local politicians jealous of the development of other states.

The problems of India's economic future are vast enough already, and many have been the prophets of woe forecasting failure. The most obvious problem is that of the huge annual increase of population, which means that a considerable proportion of any increase in the national income is swallowed up without any matching rise in per capita income. India's present population is around 470 million—the world's largest apart from that of China, and more than the total population of the Western hemisphere. Its fantastic rate of growth can be judged from the fact that it was only 356 million at the time of the 1951 census, and it is estimated that it will have reached 625 million by 1976. While there has been some reduction in the birth rate, the death rate has fallen even faster and is likely to continue to do so.

This enormous and continuing increase in population makes the conquest of the endemic poverty of India terrifyingly difficult. An annual rise in national income that would seem adequate in Western countries produces a rise in national income per head of population that scarcely seems to make an impression on chronic poverty.

National income per head in India is by no means the lowest in the world, but the poorest Indians are poor beyond the imagination of those who have not seen them. The majority of the population live in small villages, often with little or no regular communications, existing on subsistence agriculture of the most primitive kind.

It was therefore clear that a massive programme of development was necessary after independence, and that this would require both foreign aid and a big increase in internal savings and investment, to build up the economic 'infrastructure' and to press on with industrialisation and the reorganisation of agriculture. The first Five-year Plan, covering the years 1951–56, represented the beginning of this programme, but against the background of a mixed economy and with little interference in the private sector. Aided by two bumper harvests, this 'modest approach to planning'—as Mr Nehru described it—was moderately successful in increasing the national income, although it failed to live up to expectations in both industrialisation and agricultural reform.

The real difficulties began with the second Plan, covering the years 1956–61. It was avowedly aimed at remodelling the Indian economy on a socialist pattern, with great emphasis on State investment in heavy industry and a much greater measure of State control over the private sector. It envisaged not only the use of much larger quantities of foreign aid, mostly from Governments, but heavy deficit financing.

The effects were almost immediately inflationary, and the country ran at once into serious balance-of-payments difficulties which have become chronic. Indian sterling balances were heavily drawn on, foreign aid had to be stepped up, and the United States had to provide large quantities of food grains (under the PL 480 scheme) to make up for the shortfall of domestic food production and the rising prices of foodstuffs. There was a 20 per cent rise in national income over the five years, with substantial increases in heavy industrial production; but the Plan broke down badly in respect of import estimates and the costing of many major investment projects.

In the ten years to March, 1961, when the first two Plans had run their course, India's sterling balances had been reduced from some £685 million to about £102 million, while the total of foreign aid used in the same period amounted to more than £1,275 million.

The third Plan, to cover the years 1961–66, endeavoured to avoid the errors of the second. Deficit finance was to be reduced by more than half, with a still heavier reliance on foreign aid. The accent was still on mineral production and heavy industry, but agriculture, irrigation and power accounted for a larger proportion of investment outlay. Development began almost at once to fall behind projected levels, and plans were seriously complicated by the need to increase defence expenditure very heavily when the Chinese invasion threat grew more ominous.

Nevertheless, despite failure and miscalculations, despite the core of desperate individual poverty and the continuing surge of population increase, despite a chronic balance-of-payments problem, India's economic prospects were not unhopeful until the 1965 Pakistan war. Given adequate foreign aid and a successful attack on agricultural productivity through community development and co-operatives, India could reach the level of self-sustaining growth. But the Congress politicians will have to come to terms with at least one of Gandhi's legacies which was a feature of the later Five Year Plans. The insistence on cottage industries and handicrafts, largely for philosophical reasons but also in order to restrict investment in factory-made consumer goods, will certainly not meet the consumption needs of a population with a rising standard of living.

It is difficult to be sure how successful the Community Development programme has been, for the results have been distinctly patchy from one area to another. Certainly, however, many villages have been transformed, and a new relationship established between Government and people. There are many excellent and devoted public servants working in the field—but of course not nearly enough good ones.

The movement began in 1952, shortly after the inauguration of the first Five Year Plan. In October, 1959, Rajasthan was the first State to weld the Community Development system into the Gandhian system of local government, *Panchayati Raj*. It was followed by Andhra, and later by others.

This was very much the same kind of line that was being simultaneously followed in Pakistan with the merging of Community Development into the system of Basic Democracy. But *Panchayati Raj*, which had been developed in different ways and to varying degrees in different States before 1959, owes its origins to Gandhi's ideal of village democracy. The village assembly elected its *panchayat*; or if

50

the hamlet was very small, a number were grouped in Unions. It was only after the 1957 report of a committee headed by Balvantray Mehta had revealed the almost total ineffectiveness of the *panchayat* system throughout most of the country that the new system of *Panchayati Raj* began to be adopted by the States in 1959.

Briefly, the village *panchayats* elect one member each to the *Panchayat Samiti* of each Development Block (a group of about 100 villages), above which is the *Zila Parishad*, a council which brings together at District level the presidents of the *Panchayat Samitis* with executive officials and Union and State politicians.

Indians tend to get cross when comparisons are made between *Panchayati Raj* and Pakistan's Basic Democracy, for they do not concede that anything in Pakistan today can be democratic. But there seems little doubt that, whereas President Ayub Khan has succeeded in making his system work for a strictly limited purpose, the Indian system has been bedevilled over much of the country by various tensions. The *panchayats* themselves have sometimes intensified caste rivalries and resentments. The executive officials have not always been anxious to co-operate effectively with institutions which might usurp some of the power wielded by officials since the days of British rule.

Above all, the hope that *Panchayati Raj* might transcend party politics and lead to a true spirit of village community has been frustrated by the parties themselves, led by Congress. The whole system has tended to become another arena of party politics, with local party bosses and politicians involved at every turn. (President Ayub Khan, of course, averted this in his system by the totalitarian expedient of abolishing political parties altogether.)

All this has led to a revulsion against Congress party politics on the part of idealistic Gandhians like Jayaprakash Narayan, seeking to return to the village community ideal.

*　　*　　*

It was inevitable that the unassuming Mr Shastri, succeeding as a compromise candidate to the premiership, would run into political difficulties previously kept at bay by the personality and prestige of Mr Nehru. Lacking both striking personality and the heroic status of a leading 'freedom fighter' against the British, he had not at first the influence to check the separatist tendencies in the linguistic states. In his first year of office the smouldering resentment of the south against the imposition of Hindi as the official language broke out in violent rioting in Madras and Andhra, while some southern Ministers resigned from the Union Cabinet.

Bowing to *force majeure*—and no doubt influenced by the Congress Party president, the Madras leader Kamaraj Nadar —Mr Shastri suspended the time-limit and repeated Mr Nehru's pledge that English would remain an alternative official language so long as the Tamils and other non-Hindi speaking peoples wished it.

Nevertheless, the north-south conflict is still a dangerous reality, kept alive by militants on both sides. There is a strong separatist Tamil party in the south, the Dravidian Progressive Federation (DMK) founded by C. N. Annadurai. Nor is it only the language question that divides north and south. There is a colour and caste problem as well. Although seldom openly acknowledged, the dividing line between the fairer Aryans and the dark Dravidians is still real, and it is intensified by the caste division between Brahman and non-Brahman.

Hindu conservatism, like some of the policies of Gandhi, undoubtedly tends to hold back India's economic and social development. In the end, the rigidities of the caste system, still so divisive an influence, will not be able to hold out against the effects of political democracy, rising living standards among the masses and the Westernising tendencies of industrialisation. But the language problem is the most divisive of all. It must be solved if the Indian Union is to survive.

So must the endemic hostility between India and Pakistan,

still kept alive by the violent resentments engendered by the Kashmir dispute. But for these, the Rann of Kutch incident would not have occurred in 1965. Kashmir is the one issue still capable of provoking serious Hindu-Muslim clashes, and the one issue on which neither country seems capable of rational compromise. If the Indian subcontinent had to be partitioned, peace between the two component countries is essential to the progress of both. It is bad enough to have a militant imperialistic China across the border, without Indians and Pakistanis continually standing to arms against each other.

Of course, the divisions between the two countries have from the first been rendered more obvious by the alignment of Pakistan with the West and the devotion of Nehru and his followers to a neutralist 'non-alignment' policy which showed the way to Burma, Ceylon, Cambodia and for a time Indonesia. Much has been made of this policy and its significance by Western liberals—perhaps too much. It amounted to little more than a desire to stay out of the cold war— while securing much-needed economic help from both sides— and to a belief that India could do without military alliances. This belief was based partly on India's strength and the solidity of most of her frontiers, but also on a genuine conviction that no other country would attack the apostles of good will—and that if they did world opinion would destroy the aggressors. Communist China rudely shattered both these illusions. It was discovered that world opinion in the UN of today can be mobilised against former 'imperialist' powers (as when India herself helped to mobilise it at the time of Suez), but that it is much less vocal when an Asian power is the aggressor—particularly one with the influence of China.

Whether India—or, in the long run, any country in Asia— can stay wholly non-aligned will depend on the future behaviour of the Chinese. It is obvious that the Indian subcontinent needs to be defended as a whole, which makes the need for a rapprochement between India and Pakistan the more urgent.

3
India's Neighbours

PAKISTAN

FEW modern states have come into existence under more unfavourable conditions than Pakistan. Born in bloodshed and strife, it lacked material advantages. It was geographically absurd, appeared unlikely to be economically viable, and was racially as well as geographically divided. It was immediately resented by its neighbours: by India for existing at all, and thus spoiling the Indian dream of an independent and undivided sub-continent; by Afghanistan for assuming the British hegemony over the Pathans of the North West Frontier. In addition, being not a liberated dependency but only a part of one, it inherited no ready-made administrative machinery. Indeed, it lacked even a national (or nationalist) ethos, for it was not a nation.

All it possessed was the spirit of Islam, and the dynamic, revolutionary driving force of Mohammed Ali Jinnah, the 'Qaid-i-Azam' (Great Leader) of the Pakistan which his Muslim League had forced the Hindus reluctantly to concede. Pakistan was in truth the product of a revolution within a revolution; it was a revolution against the dominance of the Congress Hindus rather than against the British Raj. It was born of no racial or geographical nationalism, so that Islam became perforce its only *raison d'être*. Miraculously Pakistan has survived. Whether the partition of the sub-continent can —or ought to—endure is another question.

Divided Pakistan now consists of the eastern part of the former Province of Bengal, together with the Sylhet district of Assam, which together form the Province of East Pakistan; and a Province of West Pakistan, comprising Baluchistan, Sind, the old North West Frontier Province, the western Punjab and ten former Princely States.

The unbalanced nature of the country is shown by the population figures for the two provinces. West Pakistan (including the Federal Territory of Karachi) has an area of some 310,000 square miles and a population last estimated at 45 million. East Pakistan, little more than 55,000 square miles in area, contains more than 55 million people, having thus a population density seven times as high as that of the western province. Moreover, the population of East Bengal is probably increasing even faster than the rest.

The appalling difficulties facing the country at its birth can be judged from the fact that nearly one in every six of the original inhabitants of West Pakistan was a Muslim refugee from India. The singularly inhospitable country around Karachi became a vast camp, and the resettlement of refugees dominated the already enormous economic and social problems of Pakistan.

A controversy with India immediately arose over the question of evacuee property; this, together with the problem of control of the Indus waters, accentuated the fear and hatred of the Hindu Indians to an extent which prepared the way for the war over Kashmir.* This common fear was not enough, however, to unite Bengalis, Punjabis, Sindhis and Pathans into a nation. Even Islam was not a wholly unifying force, for there are deep splits between sects which are capable of erupting into violence, as in the 1953 Lahore clashes between orthodox Sunni and members of the Ahmadiyyah movement.

Nor was there any political *élite* capable of making a democracy work. There was a largely selfish and reactionary body of landlords, an almost medieval collection of orthodox Muslim religious leaders, and a band of lawyer-politicians who stood for very little and commanded no popular support. The British-trained Civil Service was small, overworked, and by tradition non-political. In the end, as in so many newly-independent countries, only the Army officers emerged as a capable and patriotic *élite*.

* See Chap. 2, pp. 40–42.

For years the politicians found it impossible even to draft a constitution, and from 1947 to 1956 Pakistan was governed under a modified version of the 1935 Government of India Act. Two controversies bedevilled the search for a formula. One was the question of whether the State should be secular or theocratic. Jinnah, an autocratic Governor-General, came down realistically in favour of a secular basis, but the Muslim League was divided, while the orthodox Muslim fanatics refused to give way on the issue of a religious veto.

The other controversy centred on the balance of power between East and West Pakistan. In the end a federal system was devised which created a unified province in the west out of the original medley of provinces and states, and this made it easier to balance the powers of the two Provinces at the centre. But there was also serious trouble over an attempt to impose Urdu as an official language on East Pakistan; eventually Bengali was recognised as an official language.

So long as the Qaid-i-Azam was alive, the emergency powers of the Governor-General could be used to steer the country through the prevailing political chaos. On his death in September, 1948, there was no leading figure with enough ability and prestige to rally the country. At one time it seemed as if Liaqat Ali Khan might, as Prime Minister, provide the leadership required; but he was assassinated in 1951, and there was no logical successor. In fact the Governor-General, Khawaja Nazimuddin, took over the premiership and survived until 1953 in an increasingly unstable situation. He failed dismally to cope with the serious situation created by the Lahore riots, and his successor as Governor-General, Ghulam Mohammad, dismissed him.

In October, 1954, Ghulam Mohammad also dissolved the Constituent Assembly—quite unconstitutionally—and governed by means of his reserve powers.

This situation continued until August, 1955, when the appearance on the scene of the first military 'strong man' denoted the Army's growing conviction that the time had come to take a hand if Pakistan was not to dissolve in chaos.

Major-General Iskander Mirza, the new Governor-General, was elected provisional President of the new Republic of Pakistan on March 5, 1956, a constitution having at last been agreed by a recalled Constituent Assembly. It did not last. The constitution was suspended in East Pakistan three months later, and in West Pakistan in March, 1957. It was simply impossible to secure a stable democratic government out of the warring political factions and climbing individualist politicians.

The final break with democracy occurred on October 7, 1958, when General Iskander Mirza abrogated the federal constitution. The Army's Commander-in-Chief, General Ayub Khan, was entrusted with the rule of the country under martial law. In the same month a Presidential Cabinet was appointed, consisting of twelve Ministers of whom four were Generals. Four days later General Iskander Mirza formally handed over all powers to General Ayub Khan, who assumed the office of President and confirmed the Presidential Cabinet in office. The constitution remained suspended.

The new 'Sandhurst Raj', as the military dictatorship was dubbed, inherited daunting problems and set about them with enthusiasm. As Minister for Rehabilitation, the dynamic Lieutenant-General Mohammed Azam Khan planned the resettlement of refugees (thousands of whom were still living around Karachi in the most appalling slum shanty-towns) and a massive housing programme like a military operation. Energetic and ruthless measures were taken to clean up the mess of corruption in administration left behind by the politicians, and stringent controls were imposed to halt inflation and improve the economic position. Political parties were banned and leading politicians ordered to return to private life. The lack of efficient administrators had to be made good by the drafting of Army officers into positions of responsibility. Martial law ensured the cessation of the frequent riots and demonstrations of the past.

Objectionable as all this was to the lawyer-politicians and other intellectuals, there is little doubt that the mass of the people greeted the imposition of authority with relief, if not with enthusiasm. The period of inefficiency and corruption under what purported to be a parliamentary democracy had become almost insupportable. Moreover, the Muslim ethos of Pakistan—despite the theoretical democracy of Islam—predisposes its people to a desire and respect for authority.

Nevertheless, President Ayub Khan took a clear-sighted and realistic view of the future. Faced with a somewhat similar situation in Burma, General Ne Win (who assumed office three weeks after Ayub Khan) devoted eighteen months to a 'cleaning-up operation' and then handed back power to the parliamentary politicians, only to be forced to resume it by a military *coup* two years later. The President of Pakistan clearly foresaw this danger and was determined to try to build an effective democratic system as an alternative to military dictatorship.

He rejected alike the idea of a theocratic state, since the orthodox religious leaders appeared incapable of thinking in terms of the country's present economic and social needs, and the idea that the political parties could in the near future provide stable democratic government. The Muslim League lacked both effective leadership and the prestige of the Indian Congress, while the leaders of other parties had appeared more concerned with jockeying for office than with solving the problems of Pakistan.

The President decided to build up a democratic structure from the grassroots rather than try to impose a lawyers' constitution from above. Simple in conception, the system evolved is extremely complex in structure. It is possible to say that it has worked, but still too early to say that it has succeeded, since the real test will come only when the final transfer of power to a representative government takes place. If the hideously difficult last step from autocratic to democratic rule is ultimately taken successfully, it will be a triumph owing as much to the people of Pakistan as to the strength of mind and perseverance of one man.

Before the Basic Democracy system was introduced, there already existed in Pakistan the machinery of Community Development (originally known as Village AID), administered by Government field officers with the object of stimulating agricultural modernisation and productivity. This was a paternalistic organisation which had produced some good economic results, and it was to some extent retained in the form of a National Development Organisation to provide technical services and advice. Its consultative councils, at village level and above, were absorbed into the new Basic Democracy machinery established at the end of 1959.

The avowed purpose of Basic Democracy was to find out and give graduated responsibilities to the 'natural leaders' of villages and other communities. The villagers elected Union Councils, to which were added a few members (not officials) nominated by the District Officer; small municipalities elected Town Committees. These bodies then elected their own chairmen, who formed the next tier of councils with the addition of some district officials. The chairmen of these sub-district councils were all officials, and these formed the majority of the superior District Councils, which were thus largely non-representative. The new councils were given taxing powers and charged with the duty of stimulating local economic development.

Basic Democracy, although it bore some resemblance to *Panchayati Raj* in India, was less directly representative; indeed, it was deliberately made so, in order to avoid the possibility of the Basic Democracies becoming the stamping grounds of the discredited party politicians. In addition, it lacked the parallel representative institutions of Indian parliamentary democracy, since the ultimate power in Pakistan remained firmly in the hands of the President.

Nevertheless, the search for a constitution went on. On March 1, 1962—ironically, the day before General Ne Win's forcible reassumption of power in Burma—President Ayub Khan promulgated a constitution under which the 80,000 elected members of the Basic Democracies would elect two provincial assemblies and a single-chamber federal parliament. Organised political parties were to remain proscribed, and the system of government was to be firmly presidential. The President was to appoint Ministers, control the executive and retain a power of veto. This veto was to be subject to reversal by a two-thirds majority in parliament, although the President could appeal from this to a referendum of the electoral college.

Little of this was wholly satisfactory to liberal opinion, and all of it was anathema to the ousted politicians. In fact, after the first elections the President found himself the *de facto* leader of a majority party with a divided and powerless opposition. In March, 1963, the National Assembly (meeting in Dacca, the Eastern capital, as a sop to East Pakistani feelings) wrangled for weeks about amendments to the constitution. By the time that the first general elections took place in November, 1964, the President had secured amendments which provided for the Presidential election to take place before that for Parliament, with the result that the old National Assembly would exercise the controversial power to 'screen' candidates for the Presidency who might be 'unsuitable'.

Gradually some of the 'old' politicians were allowed back into public life, but no effective leader emerged to give cohesion to an opposition consisting of five so-called parties with no significant policy or philosophy except a demand for 'democratic' institutions. The dearth of leaders was clearly demonstrated by the re-emergence from obscurity of Khawaja Nazimuddin as a temporary focus of opposition.

It was obvious, however, that he could never be an effective Presidential candidate against Ayub Khan. Finally the desperate opposition politicians persuaded Miss Fatima Jinnah, the 72-year-old sister of the Qaid-i-Azam, to lend the prestige of her (or her brother's) name to a joint opposition candidature. Miss Jinnah stood for no particular policy except opposition to the President and the restoration of direct elections, nor was she personally a very effective candidate. However, she fought an energetic and bitter campaign, and by the time polling for the electoral college ended in November, 1964, the opposition hoped that they had done well.

In the event, the electoral college returned Ayub Khan at the new year election with a landslide majority. In West Pakistan the President had a three-to-one majority, with a much smaller, but nevertheless clear, majority in the East. This even though Miss Jinnah was supported in her Eastern campaign by General Azam Khan, Ayub's former right-hand man who had achieved immense personal popularity as a vigorous Governor of East Pakistan before falling from the President's favour.

There were loud opposition complaints of interference with the freedom of the election. Some of them were probably justified, since a few of the President's local majorities looked a little too good to be true. But no impartial observer doubted that Miss Jinnah would in any case have been soundly beaten. Not only did the system favour the Field-Marshal (as he had now become), but it remained true that the majority of Pakistanis preferred a stable authority and recognised the worth of his achievements.

He still has no obvious successor. Certainly it will not be Miss Jinnah, nor any of the 'old' politicians. In recent years the Foreign Minister, Mr Z. A. Bhutto, has seemed to be emerging as the leading civilian statesman. Whether he, or anyone else, could maintain stable government after the passing of Ayub Khan, or negotiate the final hurdle of leading the country back to direct parliamentary elections, remains doubtful. And in an emergency it is fairly certain that the Army would step in again to avert chaos.

*　　*　　*

Meanwhile the economic development of Pakistan has proceeded slowly, but with a measure of success. Lacking the mineral and industrial resources of India, with poor communications and no trading contracts overseas, the country had an uphill struggle from the first. In addition, its agriculture was primitive, at the mercy of the violent floods of Bengal and the creeping menace of waterlogging and salinity in the Punjab.

Some progress has been made in the agricultural sphere, both in land reform and in flood and irrigation control, and it is likely that future progress will be more rapid. Although the industrial base of Pakistan is still small, there has been considerable development in industry. The Government has undertaken most of the 'infrastructure' development, with private enterprise playing a large part in the development of manufacturing industry. Considerable success has been achieved through the Industrial Development Corporation, a Government agency designed to initiate projects—either alone or in concert with private capital—with a view to their ultimate transfer to private investors.

Worsening terms of trade and poor overseas demand for Pakistan's staple exports of jute, tea, cotton and hides led the Government to initiate a system of export subsidies and incentives which has proved remarkably successful. Large quantities of foreign aid have been well used, and Pakistan has never been in quite the desperate foreign exchange difficulties experienced by India. National income growth has been disappointingly small, and almost entirely swallowed up by the persistent population growth, but future growth may well be more rapid as the slower-working developments in agriculture begin to bear fruit. All in all, Pakistan's economic progress, though slow and difficult, did credit to the country's Government until the 1965 Kashmir war wrecked it.

* * *

The foreign relations of Pakistan have been a source of constant anxiety. Hemmed in between a hostile India and Afghanistan, and separated from China only by Kashmir, the country's rulers never felt that they could enjoy the luxury of non-alignment. Pakistan joined SEATO in 1954 and the Baghdad Pact (later CENTO) in 1955, thus aligning herself with the West. Since neither of these organisations has ever been particularly effective or involved any serious sacrifices, this was more a gesture than a firm committal, and in fact Pakistan has tended to become less and less aligned as fences with neighbours were mended.

In 1960 the Afghan claim to the Pathan areas of the old North-West Frontier Province and Baluchistan brought the two countries to the verge of war. Indeed, there were several large-scale (and almost certainly officially supported) Afghan raids into Pakistan territory. These were backed by a political campaign which purported to appeal to the yearnings of some Pathans for an independent 'Pakhtunistan'. Finally, when Pakistan closed down Afghan consulates and trading agencies in the north-west as centres of subversion, Afghanistan broke off diplomatic relations and trade with Pakistan in September, 1961. The cessation of the very considerable flow of Afghan exports through the port of Karachi did both countries great economic harm. Afghan internal propaganda against Pakistan was again stepped up, and only the fact that Pakistani regular forces and tribal levies proved more than a match for raiding Afghans prevented a major invasion.

Relations did not improve until Sardar Mohammed Daud, the King's first cousin, was replaced as Prime Minister of Afghanistan by Dr Mohammed Yusuf. In May, 1963, after anxious mediation by the United States and Persia, a conference in Tehran resulted in the resumption of diplomatic and trading relations with Pakistan.

This made it easier for Pakistan to improve relations with Soviet Russia, which she has since done. More obvious, however, has been the growing rapprochement with China, stimulated by a common hostility to India. China has virtually guaranteed the frontier with Pakistan-controlled Azad ('Free') Kashmir, and relations have become markedly closer, culminating in a visit to Pakistan by Chou En-lai in 1965.

Pakistan remains overtly aligned in the Western alliance, while constantly protesting against the volume of Western arms aid to India. The situation brought about by the Kashmir dispute is, of course, a constant source of embarrassment to the United Kingdom and the United States. These countries find themselves obliged to aid non-aligned India with arms to defend herself against communist China, while their indignant aligned ally Pakistan complains that these arms are likely to be used against herself.

Both Britain and the US have tried to mediate in the Kashmir dispute, and helped to bring about a long series of negotiations in 1963. Both India and Pakistan remained intransigent. Neither Mr Nehru nor the Indian Army was disposed to yield an inch. Pakistan held out for a plebiscite in the Indian-controlled Valley of Kashmir, knowing that this would almost certainly result in a vote in favour of accession to Pakistan—although the longer India continued her policy of deliberately rapid development and economic aid the smaller the majority would probably be.

The situation has been periodically complicated and exacerbated by the independent campaign for Kashmiri self-determination waged by the former Chief Minister Sheikh Abdullah. Released from prison by Mr Nehru in April, 1964, he was banished to South India by Mr Shastri in May, 1965. This step was followed by disorders in Indian Kashmir and an intensification of Pakistani activity on the cease-fire line which flared up again into a shooting war. In fact, Kashmir is partitioned between India, Pakistan and China, which invaded Ladakh and refused to leave.

It must probably be taken as a dismal political fact of life that in present circumstances no Indian or Pakistani government could afford to yield much in the Kashmir dispute, which remains one of the supreme tragic nonsenses of the world. It is little short of appalling that this dispute should keep the two nations of the sub-continent in a state of continual preparation for war against each other. Both are poor countries, ill able to afford the defence budgets needed to 'secure' themselves against each other. Ultimately common sense demands that India and Pakistan shall come to some sort of rapprochement, leading to common policies in external affairs. Russian diplomacy at the Tashkent Conference in January, 1966, may have provided a new basis for future talks.

TIBET AND NEPAL

Beyond the Himalaya and Nepal lies Tibet, largely a vast plateau 16,000 ft above sea-level. Of Mongol origin, with a language allied to that of the Burmans, the Tibetans have had a long history, during much of which they rivalled the Afghans in the skilled playing-off of one great power against another without sacrificing their essential independence.

Early in the seventh century A.D. Tibet became a powerful state. Its king, Song-tsen Gam-po, founded the capital of Lhasa and introduced Buddhism from India. In the middle of the thirteenth century much of Tibet was conquered by Kublai Khan, who is said to have initiated the theocratic rule of the lamas. Tibet remained more or less independent until 1720, when the first Manchu Emperor of China took Lhasa. Thereafter, until the Chinese revolution of 1912, the Manchu dynasty claimed suzerainty over Tibet, although it gradually became more and more nominal.

British interest in Tibet goes back as far as the Indian Governor-Generalship of Warren Hastings. The Government of British India remained anxious to organise trade across the frontier, and to demarcate the frontier itself; but the Tibetans remained elusive, and no representative of the British or Indian Governments succeeded in penetrating to Lhasa. However, in 1888 the Chinese invaded Sikkim, an exploit which their communist descendants were to repeat some 75 years later. The British Indian Army drove them out, and the Indian and Chinese Governments concluded an agreement demarcating the frontier between India and Tibet.

This agreement the Tibetans, who had not been made a party to it, refused to recognise, and frontier incursions became frequent. China, whose writ had virtually ceased to run in Tibet, was unable to secure observance of the treaty. Finally Colonel (later Sir Francis) Younghusband succeeded in making contact, but was unable to reach any agreement with the Dalai Lama, who was busy negotiating with Russia. In 1904 a military expedition from India took Lhasa after some hard fighting, and a treaty was signed which fixed the frontier with India and gave Britain certain trading concessions. Both China and Russia later concluded agreements with Britain which secured the virtual neutralisation of Tibet. But no sooner had the British evacuated the country than the Chinese annexed it, and it remained at least nominally a province of China until the revolution, when the Tibetans threw the Chinese out by force and reinstated the Dalai Lama at Lhasa. The revolutionary Chinese Government never accepted this *fait accompli*, and tried to reconquer the country. In 1912 an expedition was withdrawn after a strong British reaction, and in 1918 the Tibetans fought off another.

Subsequent British and Indian attempts to secure firm Chinese agreement on the autonomy of Tibet failed, and in October, 1950, the so-called Chinese People's Liberation Army invaded Tibet and (the UN having failed to respond to Tibetan appeals) re-established the suzerainty of China over the country, leaving the control of internal affairs still nominally in the hands of the Dalai Lama.

In fact, the Chinese proceeded to attempt the reorganisation of the country along communist lines, which were far from compatible with the theocratic nature of lamaism—as had been demonstrated in Mongolia in the 1920s. In 1959 the Tibetans, led by the Khamba tribe, revolted. The rising was bloodily suppressed, although pockets of resistance probably still survive, and the Dalai Lama fled to seek sanctuary in India, subjecting Mr Nehru's non-alignment to a severe strain. The Panchen Lama, his spiritual counterpart, was installed as puppet ruler of a Tibet which was now to all intents and purposes incorporated into communist China.

Thus was consummated an uneasy relationship between Tibet and China which had lasted for 700 years, since the time of the Great Khan. Various Chinese Governments had signed various agreements guaranteeing various degrees of independence to Tibet; but the claim to suzerainty was never abandoned, and the Chinese imperialist ethos remains unchanged by Marxist-Leninist dogma. Almost certainly no effective Chinese Government will ever relinquish Tibet voluntarily or be ejected from it by outside force. If Tibet is ever to regain its freedom, it will only be by internal revolt against a disintegrating government.

Meanwhile, China now has a frontier with India, and a disputed frontier at that. The dispute has elements of irony which would be almost funny if the implications were not so serious. Independent India takes her stand on the so-called MacMahon Line, negotiated with China and Tibet in 1914 by the former colonial power. The Chinese deny the validity of the agreement, which indeed China had never ratified. Further, after the Chinese invasion of north-east India in September, 1962, it began to become apparent that neither side was absolutely sure where, in places, the MacMahon Line was.

In all probability there is genuine uncertainy as to where the whole frontier between India and Tibet lies in the mountains. But it is a dispute that could be easily resolved, given genuine willingness on the Chinese side. So far, this has not been apparent.

*   *   *

The communist Chinese annexation of Tibet transformed the significance of the Kingdom of Nepal, a mountain state of some 54,000 square miles and more than 9 million inhabitants, which lies between Tibet and the Ganges Plain of India. It is a fertile agricultural land, with productive forests as well as pastoral and arable country. The people are of mixed race, the original Mongol stock having been much infiltrated by Indian blood. Hinduism and Buddhism flourish side by side. Among the many tribes of Nepal the Gurkha, later to provide many thousands of magnificent mercenary soldiers for the Indian and British Armies, became dominant in the middle of the eighteenth century.

Nepal awoke from a century of feudal exploitation after Indian independence. Despite the nominal suzerainty of British India and the existence of a royal family of Rajput extraction, Nepal had been for a century almost entirely owned and governed by one immense and powerful family, the Ranas. His Highness Sir Padma Shamsher Jang Bahadur Rana called himself Maharaja of Nepal, and was in fact Prime Minister and Commander-in-Chief. The top Ranas, to whom the senior military and administrative posts were reserved by prescriptive family right, were fabulously wealthy and lived like medieval princes. Even the offspring of their many concubines were eligible for promotion in the lower reaches of the racket.

To the nominal suzerainty over this Arabian Nights anachronism Mr Nehru became the embarrassed heir in 1947. There was already in being a Nepali National Congress party founded in January, 1946, and supported by Jayaprakash Narayan and other Congress Indians. It must have seemed likely to Mr Nehru and his friends that this party would ultimately overthrow the Ranas and that Nepal would live happily ever after in a close relationship with Mother India. Events worked out in a startlingly different way.

Early in 1947 the Maharaja Padma perceived the writing on the wall. He sought to establish contact with China, secured from the United States a recognition of Nepal's independence, and announced a number of liberal reforms including a measure of democracy based on a *panchayat* system. He then, on May 1, 1948, resigned while the going was good and retired to enjoy his wealth in India. His successor, H.H. Maharaja Mohan Shamsher Jang Bahadur Rana, reaped the whirlwind.

Political agitation increased. The Nepali National Congress merged with the Nepal Democratic Congress, a party founded in 1948 by dissatisfied illegitimate Ranas, to form the Nepali Congress. Its President was M. P. Koirala, whose half-brother B. P. Koirala was a much-imprisoned NNC agitator. At the end of September, 1950, the Government purported

68

to discover a conspiracy which necessitated the arrest of leading politicians in the capital (Katmandu). The Nepali Congress prepared for the final battle for freedom.

It was forestalled. On November 6 the forgotten King Tribhuvana, hitherto virtually a captive puppet of the Ranas, suddenly came to life. He escaped with the Crown Prince Mahendra to the Indian Embassy, and thence to New Delhi. The Government's attempt to place the King's infant grandson on the throne and carry on as before was followed by a NC invasion from India. This was suppressed by the Army, but the end was in sight. The NC, however, was out-manœuvred. The King returned to Katmandu in triumph, appointed his own Council including Rana and NC Ministers and summoned a Constituent Assembly to evolve a democratic constitution. Maharaja Mohan Rana remained Prime Minister.

For a time there was political chaos. Parties grew up like mushrooms, until there were more than thirty, some of them led by almost forgotten 'freedom fighters' released from prison after ten or twenty years. The communists, too, became active. In November, 1951, Mohan Rana was forced to resign, and M. P. Koirala became the first non-Rana Prime Minister of Nepal.

Chaos continued. Between November, 1951, and May, 1959, there were nine Governments, all appointed by the King. In March, 1955, King Tribhuvana died; his successor Mahendra, a taciturn but purposeful young man of 35, played things along much as before—awaiting his moment.

Democracy was given a chance. The long awaited Constitution appeared in 1959, and a general election duly gave the NC a parliamentary majority in the Lower House, carefully balanced by royal appointments to the Upper. B. P. Koirala, who had fallen out with his half-brother, became Prime Minister and failed to hit it off with the King. There were disorders in the country, and communist activity increased.

In December, 1960, the King carried out a sudden *coup*,

dissolved Parliament, arrested most of the politicians and assumed all the powers of government. Political parties were banned and plans proclaimed for a grassroots system of *panchayat* democracy.

Mr Nehru expressed himself as dismayed by this 'setback to democracy', and Indo-Nepali relations cooled. They were not improved by the activities of NC politicians who had fled to India, nor by the King's successful attempts to open cordial relations with China and Pakistan.

In October, 1961, India received a major shock, when an agreement was announced whereby China was to build by 1966 the Nepal section of a major motor road linking Katmandu with Lhasa, thus providing the Chinese with a strategic route into India. By a strange coincidence, there was an outbreak of rebel activity in early 1962, organized from NC headquarters in Calcutta.

The King was not, however, walking into the carefully baited trap of Chinese domination. Having taken a long, cool look at his country's situation, he had decided to lessen Nepal's economic dependence on India; he became not just non-aligned, but non-aligned in as many directions as possible. Foreign aid began to flow in from both East and West, and the modernisation of Nepal was under way.

Despite the umbrage of ex-politicians and dispossessed Ranas, despite Indian disapproval and communist agitation, the King's personal popularity in Nepal increased. Venerated by the masses as a reincarnation of Vishnu, he succeeded also in making it clear to the increasing numbers of educated young people that his policies were working and the future prospects of the country improving.

In the long run the links of history and geography were bound to bring India and Nepal back into amity. India is essential to Nepal and, with the Chinese on the Himalaya, a friendly Nepal is a strategic necessity for India. After the Chinese invasions of north-east India, in which King Mahendra remained scrupulously neutral (although thousands of Gurkha mercenaries were fighting in the Indian Army), fences were mended. In August, 1963, the King paid a State visit to India, after which President Radhakrishnan was received with great cordiality in Katmandu.

Nepal has thus reverted to her ancient—and not unprofitable—role of neutrality between India and China. The Chinese appear to be making no claims to suzerainty, nor would India and her Western supporters allow the absorption of Nepal. There is still a danger from internal communist subversion, but King Mahendra's position seems secure. Nepal may have to wait a long time for the arrival of that blessed state of democracy which Congress so confidently expected, but her swift stride from Rana feudalism into the modern world is an achievement of which the King may well be proud.

CEYLON

The transfer of power in newly independent colonial territories is generally preceded by a period of increasingly militant nationalist agitation. The colonial power, making reluctant concessions, fixes a 'safe' date for independence in the future and then has to expedite the process to avoid intolerable strain. Power is then transferred to the most militant nationalist leader, amid pessimistic prognostications of disaster from the colonialists.

It was quite otherwise with Ceylon. The island had by 1948 already become much more nearly self-governing than most colonies, and it slid almost imperceptibly into independence under impeccably conservative and westernised leaders. Everything seemed to be set fair for a tranquil future, and for the first eight years the promise appeared to be fulfilled. Nobody foresaw that Ceylon would become the problem child of the Commonwealth, politically unstable and economically bankrupt.

With the benefit of hindsight, it is perhaps possible to deduce the reasons for the *débâcle*, and even to suspect that the seeds of disaster lay in the very things that seemed so reassuring in 1948. There was no 'struggle' for independence to serve as an outlet for nationalist feelings. Nationalism lay dormant and unsatisfied; when it broke out, the vessel was not strong enough to contain the ferment.

The island of Ceylon (Sri Lanka in Sinhalese) lies to the south of India and is rather more than 25,000 square miles in area. The population has increased from some 7¼ million at independence to around 10½ million and is of mixed races. About 65 per cent of the people are Sinhalese, of whom the Kandyan Sinhalese can be distinguished from those of the low-country districts. Roughly 10 per cent are Ceylon Tamils, of southern Indian stock but nationals of Ceylon, and about another 10 per cent are Indian Tamils mostly working on plantations. The only other large group is the 'Moors', Muslims of Arabic descent.

The Sinhalese, whose language is of Aryan Indian descent, are for the most part Buddhists. The Tamils, speaking their native Dravidian dialect, are mostly Hindus.

According to the Asian pattern of gradual southward drift, one would have expected to find Ceylon being first colonised by Dravidians from southern India, with the northern Aryans seeking to penetrate later. The reverse seems to have been the case. Whoever were the aboriginal inhabitants of the island, it was colonised by people from the Ganges valley as early as the sixth century B.C. Indeed the first King of the Sinhalese is reputed to have been an Indian prince from the north named Vijaya, who ruled from the middle of the sixth century. That some cultural links with the north were retained is suggested by the fact that Buddhism was introduced into Ceylon in the third century B.C., at a time when it was spreading rapidly in the northern empire of Asoka.

The Tamils from southern India were the later invaders, and many of the early Sinhalese national heroes won their laurels fighting against them. This historical fact is important today because it has undoubtedly aggravated the inter-racial tensions since the belated outburst of Sinhalese nationalism.

The first European lodgment was made in 1505 by the

Portuguese, who established commercial settlements in the south and west. Although the Portuguese remained for only 150 years, before being dispossessed by the Dutch, their impact was considerable and their memory is preserved not only in the name of the capital Colombo but in the Sinhalese families of de Silva, Perera, de Zoysa and many others.

As in the East Indies, Britain took advantage of the French conquest of Holland to wrest the Ceylon settlements from the Dutch in 1795, and in this case forgot to give them back. Ruled for a time from Madras, they became a British Crown Colony in 1801. The customary process of expansion disposed in 1815 of the central highland Kingdom of Kandy, which had existed for some 23 centuries, and the whole of Ceylon became a British colony.

The progress towards self-government started as early as 1833, when a Legislative Council (with no effective powers) included some nominated Ceylonese members. From 1912 onwards the Legislative Council was progressively enlarged and made increasingly elective, until in 1931 a new constitution (largely the work of the Donoughmore Commission of 1927-28) introduced universal adult franchise for the election by territorial constituencies of fifty representatives, who with twelve nominated representatives of other interests formed a new State Council with legislative and executive functions. This constitution survived until independence in February, 1948, when the new Commonwealth country adopted a parliamentary system of two chambers and Cabinet, with a Governor-General as head of state.

In the earlier colonial days, such representation as there was in the government of Ceylon had been carefully balanced by the British to give the Tamils and other minorities rather more than their numerical share. Under the Donoughmore Constitution the Sinhalese gradually collected the reins of power, largely held by members of the Goyigama caste under the leadership of D. S. Senanayake. Nevertheless, when Senanayake became Ceylon's first Prime Minister in 1948, he was leading a United National Party which included Ceylon Tamils and Muslims.

Although political leadership was firmly in the hands of a Western-educated, English-speaking *élite*—representative neither of Sinhalese nationalist feeling nor of the communalism and caste divisions of the people—it is possible that Senanayake might have succeeded in his ambition to unite the people of Ceylon into a nation. He was probably the one man who could have done it; but he died in 1952, and his party began to break up. He was succeeded as Prime Minister by his son Dudley, who resigned in 1953 after a national crisis provoked by the unpopular (though probably economically sound) removal of the rice subsidy. The next Premier was D. S. Senanayake's nephew, Sir John Kotelawala, a good administrator but neither popular nor inspired.

In the elections of 1956 the UNP was crushingly defeated by a coalition formed by S.W.R.D. Bandaranaike out of Sinhalese nationalists and left-wing groups. The victory of his Sri Lanka Freedom Party and its allies was the *tour de force* of a very shrewd politician who had seen which way the wind was blowing in Ceylon.

It was not only that the UNP had been in power too long and had no new ideas. There was a revulsion of Sinhalese nationalist feeling against the old English-educated political *élite*, with their Western manners and English Christian names. There was also increasing hostility to the industrious Tamils, both on economic grounds and because their Indian origins and connections seemed to threaten the integrity of Ceylon. Bandaranaike pandered to the growing anti-Western feeling (although he came from the old *élite* himself), to the anti-Tamil feeling, and to the marked revival of Buddhist devotion. He promised to restore Buddhism to its old importance, to promote a revival of Sinhalese culture, and to make Sinhalese the official language. He also combined an appeal to the Left with an appeal to anti-Western sentiment by promising both to nationalise foreign-owned plantations and to end 'military agreements with the imperialists' (which

74

meant abrogating both the British alliance and the agreement to preserve the British naval base at Trincomalee).

Having uncorked the bottle, Bandaranaike found it less easy to control the genie he had released. The nationalist ferment broke out in terrible communal rioting in 1956 and 1958, religious fanaticism increased, and the Marxists in the Government coalition (led by the Trotskyist Philip Gunawardena) became so militant that they had to be dropped. Not long afterwards Bandaranaike was assassinated by a Buddhist monk.

After a caretaker government interlude under W. Dahanayake, a general election in March, 1960, returned the UNP as the largest single party but without a working majority. Dudley Senanayake's government was soon defeated, and another election in July, 1960, gave the SLFP a conclusive victory. The new Prime Minister was Mrs Bandaranaike, widow of the 'martyred' SLFP leader. Her Cabinet appeared to be dominated by her husband's nephew, F. R. D. Bandaranaike, the Finance Minister.

The new Government pushed ahead with the old Bandaranaike policies. Partly as a result of the communal troubles caused by the increasing dissatisfaction of the Tamils with oppressive legislation and the imposition of Sinhalese as the national language, and partly owing to costly welfare measures and nationalisation, the economic situation grew steadily more desperate. Budget deficits mounted, the balance-of-payments position became acute, and foreign capital was effectively frightened away. Disorders were common, and the Government resorted to emergency powers, illegal arrests and drastic action to curb strikes.

By the middle of 1964 Mrs Bandaranaike's parliamentary majority was in danger, and she had to come to an agreement with the Trotskyists. As part of the deal, she undertook to introduce legislation for what amounted to nationalisation and Government control of the independent (and hostile) Press. In the event, she found herself unable to deliver the goods, owing to violent opposition.

On December 3, her Government was unexpectedly defeated in Parliament by one vote. Mrs Bandaranaike hung on for a week, while Colombo buzzed with rumours that further unconstitutional actions were in prospect. In the end, however, she capitulated and asked the Governor-General for a dissolution. A general election in March, 1965, put Mr Dudley Senanayake back in office with a UNP majority.

Apart from the endemic problems of communalism and language—the Tamils are now politically organised in a Federalist group with a separatist platform—his problems were overwhelmingly economic. There were soon signs that foreign aid and capital would be more readily available for a policy of removing some of the restrictions from private enterprise and making public enterprise more a spur to development than a welfare prop. But Ceylon has still a long way to go, and many difficult internal problems to surmount.

4
Burma

BURMA is a country of crucial strategic importance in Southeast Asia, lying as it does between India and China, between Thailand and China, and covering virtually the whole eastern coastline of the Bay of Bengal. It not only offers a route from China to the Ganges Plain, but also consists largely of river valleys running north and south from the borders of China to the Bay of Bengal.

The area of Burma is just over 260,000 square miles, or nearly one-fifth of the size of India; but Burma's population is only some 21 million, less than one-twentieth of the size of India's. Although the Burman* majority rules, more than 40 per cent of the inhabitants of Burma belong to racial minorities, mostly localised and some of them strong and self-conscious. This is one reason—though by no means the only one—for the chronic political and economic weakness of Burma since independence.

Until about 2,000 years ago, Burma was probably an almost uninhabited tract of jungle forests, with no more than a few aboriginal tribesmen—the ancestors of the Andamanese. It then began to be penetrated by Indo-Aryans from India, who settled colonies in the south. Then began what has been the main (and still continuing) infiltration, that of Mongolian tribes moving southward from the mountains of China into the river valleys of Burma. The first, probably, were the Karens and the Mons (Talaings), followed by the more numerous Tibeto-Burmans. Centuries later began the great expansion of the Shans—who are the same race as the Thais and Laos—from their kingdom of Nanchao in Yunnan. They spread into Assam, Siam, Indo-China and Burma, where they

---

* 'Burman' is here used as an ethnic term, 'Burmese' for all nationals of Burma.

temporarily swamped the other races, founding a number of petty kingdoms which dominated the country during the fourteenth and fifteenth centuries. They were followed into Burma by the Chins and Kachins, together with some minor tribes.

The early Indian culture in Burma had been Brahman, but Buddhism not only replaced this but gained ground rapidly among the Mongolian races, who were Animists (as some of their descendants still are). Hinayana Buddhism, which probably reached Burma from Ceylon, developed as the main religion of the country from the eleventh century, when Anawrahta—who as the first unifier of Burma has a historical reputation rather like that of Alfred the Great—suppressed in Upper Burma the corrupt form of the Mahayana cult practised there.

The dynasty established by Anawrahta at Pagan lasted for 230 years, until in 1287 Kublai Khan's Tartars destroyed it and left Burma open to the Shans. For 500 years Burma was never more than briefly united, and the power of the various races—Burmans, Shans and Mons— fluctuated from generation to generation, Portuguese mercenaries playing some part in the sixteenth and seventeenth centuries. In the middle of the eighteenth century the Mons came within an ace of securing control of Upper Burma, capturing Ava, the Burman capital. But the Burman King Alaungpaya drove them out and finally gained control of the entire Irrawaddy valley and of Pegu. He established the port of Rangoon and united the country under Burman control, under which it remained until his successors, having conquered Arakan and invaded Manipur and Assam, confronted the British on the frontiers of Bengal.

In 1824, Burmese forces were preparing to attack Chittagong, and the British East India Company either became alarmed for the safety of Bengal or decided that it had an adequate excuse for extending its empire eastwards (according to what view one takes about British imperialism). At any rate, the British won the First Burmese War, securing not

78

only Assam and Manipur but the whole coastal area of Burma except the Irrawaddy delta. In fact, this first conquest can be attributed almost entirely to strategic motives. While leaving the body of Upper and Lower Burma intact, it did secure the frontiers of Bengal; at the same time, the cession of Tenasserim placed the British in a strategic position on the borders of Siam and brought their power down to the vital Kra Isthmus where they could guard the approaches to the Malayan peninsula, in which Raffles had already established the beginnings of British influence.

The Burmese Government at Ava, however, did not take kindly to British expansion, and relations were never friendly. In 1852–53 the second Anglo-Burmese War resulted in the conquest of Lower Burma. Only Upper Burma, with its capital now at Mandalay, remained independent, the last years of the royal dynasty being marked by a series of palace revolts and family massacres. By now, the main interest of the British in Burma was trade; the Burmese, however, were not unnaturally deeply suspicious of any British attempts to expand their influence into Upper Burma, and King Thibaw tried to bring in French trading interests as a countercheck. The British promptly captured Mandalay in 1885 and deported Thibaw to India.

Although the Kingdom of Burma had finally been destroyed, it took the British about ten years to establish their rule over the whole country. Upper Burma was in chaos, existing bands of dacoits having been reinforced by Thibaw's army, while the Kachins conducted periodical forays from the north. In five years Upper Burma and the Shan States in the east were brought under control, but the Kachins did not submit until 1895 nor the Chins and the Eastern Karens till 1896.

*   *   *

Argument over the balance-sheet of British achievement in Burma is virtually endless. Many Englishmen who spent most of their lives there still maintain stoutly that the

79

economic development of Burma and the establishment of the rule of law were magnificent achievements, and that without the British the country would have remained primitive, lawless and been even poorer. They refuse to ascribe the troubles of Burma since independence to any defects of British rule, attributing them in part to the ravages of war and in part to the removal of British rule itself. The British, they say, would not only have restored the economy but also avoided the debilitating struggles of racial minorities against the Burman government.

On the other hand, extreme Burmese nationalists attribute nearly all the country's troubles to previous British exploitation and suppression.

It is impossible to do more here than attempt a very brief assessment of the balance of argument, and the verdict must surely be that Britain's half-century of dominion over a united Burma was very far from being one of her greatest successes. Not only was the economic development of the country carried out at the cost of the disintegration of traditional Burmese society, but it actually increased economic instability among the Burmese peoples themselves. The economy was certainly able to support a much larger population, but it is very doubtful whether real standards of living increased; there is some evidence that they actually fell.

Burma was, in fact, economically exploited by the British; and, while the British did not in fact pocket all, or perhaps even the majority, of the profits, the Burmese got almost nothing. Even the blessings of law and order were always less evident in Burma than in other colonial territories, for dacoity was never wholly suppressed and the crime rate seems to have remained the highest in South-east Asia, to say nothing of a degree of corruption unusual under a British administration.

Moreover, the British seem to have been much less successful in achieving satisfactory personal and social relationships with the Burmese than with other peoples. There was no western-educated aristocracy and only a tiny intellectual *élite*, in marked contrast to the situation in India, and this no doubt intensified the isolation of a small British community which appears to have been singularly insular and tactless by any standards. It seems scarcely credible today that the simple custom of removing the shoes, even on entering a Buddhist temple, was considered too degrading for the British in Burma to stomach. This shibboleth, which was worrying English envoys to the old Burmese court before the conquest, was so potent that Diana Duff Cooper reported in 1941 that none of her British friends in Rangoon had ever been inside the magnificent Shwe Dagon Pagoda.

The British did not even succeed in uniting Burma into a nation, as the risings of Karens, Mons, Shans and other minorities against a Burman government after independence clearly showed. The Karens, who, being an industrious race with a high proportion of Christians, had enjoyed a rather special relationship with the British and formed the backbone of the Burmese army, had never lost their distrust of the Burmans; the other non-Burman hill tribes on the frontiers had always been under direct British rule and insulated from the rest of the country.

*   *   *

The Burmese social order had been based on a combination of feudal administration and Buddhist culture and education. The British broke up the old feudal system and discouraged the influence of the Buddhist monks, whose discipline and educational standards began to decline.

It can hardly be doubted, however, that the fundamental error of the British was the initial decision to administer Burma as part of the Indian Empire, which resulted in virtually uncontrolled Indian immigration into the country. It was not until 1937 that Burma ceased to be a province of British India and became a Dominion with a Governor directly responsible to London.

The Indians, particularly the Chettyar moneylenders, came near to destroying the Burmese peasantry in Lower Burma, while Indian coolies continually depressed the wage levels of Burmese workers. The British developed teak forestry, and later the oil and other mineral industries, but the main development was the enormous expansion of rice production and exports from the Irrawaddy delta and basin. Whereas in most Asian colonies agricultural exports were generally developed by European plantation companies employing local wage labour, while the bulk of the rural population were engaged in peasant subsistence farming, the huge cash crops of the Burma rice bowl were raised by Burmese peasants.

This apparently favourable situation did not, however, benefit the Burmese, owing to the *laisser-faire* economic philosophy of the government, which controlled neither agricultural credit arrangements nor the alienation of land. Rice production increased vastly and rapidly, but at the cost of a steadily increasing peasant indebtedness to the Chettyars, who secured the ownership of more and more land from farmers unable to pay their debts. It was estimated that by 1930 Indians owned something like £50 million worth of property in Burma—an amount slightly larger than the whole of the controlling British investment in all the other industries of the country together.

The open exploitation of Burma and the Burmese by British and Indians—not to mention the Chinese—provoked considerable dissatisfaction and unrest, culminating in riots and rebellion in 1930, when the world depression of commodity prices caused great hardship to the now largely landless Burmese peasants. But this discontent had as yet no political focus and little leadership, for Burmese politics were already displaying the incoherence and fissiparous tendencies that have become almost chronic.

The genesis of party politics in Burma is to be found in the appearance, in 1908, of the Young Men's Buddhist Association. Founded in imitation of the YMCA, this was not intended to be in the least a political body, but it provided the only focus of organisation for young Burman nationalists. (The non-Burman races were never, because of their distrust

of the Burman majority, unreservedly in favour of the independence of a united Burma.) Between the wars the
nationalists split again and again, largely on the issue of
separation from India; many believed that Burma would
never achieve independence on her own, while the strength
of the Indian National Congress might secure the independence of both countries. In the event, the Japanese solved the
problem.

Two Burman politicians emerged from the welter of
nationalist factions disputing for office during the period
from 1937 to 1941, when the new constitution provided a
limited measure of self-government with a number of important powers reserved to the Governor. They were Ba Maw,
a Western-educated lawyer who became the first Prime
Minister of Burma in 1937, and U (=Mr) Saw, a home-
educated demagogue who succeeded to the premiership
in 1939. Neither of these ambitious leaders achieved a very
large popular following, and both subsequently became involved with the Japanese.

Meanwhile the nationalist leaders who were ultimately to
be the most influential in Burma were making their mark
in student politics at Rangoon University. In 1935 U Nu, a
post-graduate law student, was elected president of the
students' union, while Aung San became its secretary. These
two extreme nationalists, who organised a students' strike
in 1936, became leading members of a left-wing group who
called themselves Thakins (masters).

*   *   *

In view of the distinctly moderate enthusiasm for British
rule in Burma—at least among the Burmans—it is hardly
surprising that the outbreak of the Second World War provoked little loyal enthusiasm and much calculation among the
nationalists as to how events could be turned to their advantage. Ba Maw and the Thakins did their best, by threatening
to sabotage the war effort, to blackmail the British into promising independence. Ba Maw and some of his young

associates were imprisoned, but a number of Thakins fled to the Japanese, whom they already saw as the potential liberators of Burma from the British.

It is easy enough to believe that they, and other Burmese politicians who at first supported the Japanese cause, were excessively simple-minded; it is less reasonable to accuse them, as the British naturally did, of 'disloyalty'. The Burmese nationalists could not, by definition, feel any loyalty to Britain, and they had no confidence at all in the professional Rangoon politicians, whom they regarded as being either British puppets or corrupt careerists. They did not believe that the British had any intention of granting them early independence unless coerced (in which they may well have been right), and their sympathies were naturally more inclined towards an Asian power than towards Europeans. Ever since the Russo-Japanese War, Japan had been something of an inspiration to the nationalists of South-east Asia.

In 1941 U Saw visited London to make one more attempt to wrest from the British Government a promise of independence after the war, this time promising full Burmese co-operation in the war effort as a *quid pro quo*. He failed to obtain this assurance, and on his way home entered into negotiations with the Japanese. The British, however, discovered this, and he was arrested and imprisoned overseas for the rest of the war.

Japan's initial success after her declaration of war on the Allies convinced the Burmese nationalists that they were indeed beholding the rising sun of Asia. The fall of Singapore in February, 1942, marked the end of European prestige and supremacy in Asia—as it also marked the end of Australasian confidence in Britain's ability to defend the outposts of Empire. European rule and influence were based on an implicit belief in the ultimate sanction of force; once this was shattered, the end was in sight. When the Japanese entered Burma, they came with the enthusiastic support and assistance of all the extreme Burmese nationalists. Ba Maw, released from prison, was established by the Japanese conquerors as head of the puppet government of a nominally 'independent' Burma; in this government U Nu was Foreign Minister and Aung San Minister of Defence.

They were not long in discovering their error. Even before it became obvious that Japan was going to lose the war, it was abundantly clear that the Japanese did not regard their fellow-Asians as equals to be granted genuine independence. It was equally plain that they could teach even the Chettyars a trick or two when it came to exploitation. The Thakins, having reached positions of influence through co-operation with the Japanese, remained determined to achieve the reality of independence. Than Tun, Minister of Agriculture, was the first Thakin to become a resistance leader, in middle Burma in March, 1945. There were already communist units in Arakan, and Karens fighting in the east.

Aung San, now the acknowledged leader of the Thakins, laid his plans carefully. Under cover of the loudly pro-Japanese Ba Maw régime, which had declared war on the Allies, he developed an anti-Japanese resistance movement which became the Anti-Fascist People's Freedom League, ultimately the dominant political force in Burma. As soon as it became clear that the Japanese had lost the war, he emerged in yet another guise as Major-General Aung San, commander of the Burma National Army, and offered to collaborate with the Allies against the Japanese.

When the British regained control of Burma, Aung San and AFPFL were in a position of dominant political advantage. The British scarcely knew what to make of them. The civilian officials profoundly distrusted them: were they not anti-British, former collaborators with the Japanese, left-wing socialists (those who were not communists), dedicated to immediate Burmese independence and hostile to British trading interests? The military authorities, however, saw the realities of the situation more clearly, and it was Admiral Mountbatten who came down decisively for co-operation and averted an immediate clash. Even after the Japanese surrender, when there was a Labour Government in Britain, it was touch-and-go whether Aung San was arrested—which would certainly have provoked a general rising against the British.

In the event, after a convincing display of power involving a series of paralysing strikes, Aung San succeeded not only in establishing his right to recognition as the dominant Burmese leader but also in greatly accelerating the British timetable for the granting of independence. At the beginning of 1947 he reached an agreement with the British Government which was ratified by the AFPFL, although it was opposed by U Saw, now released from custody and ambitious for personal power. Elections for a Constituent Assembly gave Aung San a large majority, which decided that Burma should become an independent republic. Negotiations continued about the position of the minority races, the Karens in particular demanding strong safeguards—if not independence on their own. The communists were, for reasons not entirely motivated by concern for Burmese national interests, hostile to the constitutional proposals as a whole.

On July 19, 1947, a tragedy occurred which changed the whole history of Burma. Aung San and six of his Cabinet colleagues were assassinated by agents of his rival U Saw. There is little doubt that Aung San was more able, experienced and politically skilful than the other nationalist leaders, and none at all that he towered above them in popular esteem. He would almost certainly have become one of the great charismatic leaders of Asia. Whether he would have been successful in solving the problems of his country and holding its centrifugal forces together is another question; but he would undoubtedly have started with unequalled advantages, and he was utterly ruthless in pursuit of his aims.

U Saw did not benefit from the murders he procured, and was indeed tried and executed for them in the following year. The Governor had immediately filled Aung San's place by nominating the latter's lieutenant U Nu as Prime Minister, and a breakdown was temporarily averted by the support accorded him by the communists under Aung San's brother-in-law Than Tun. The respite lasted long enough for the

86

agreement with the British to be carried through, and Burma duly became an independent republic in January, 1948.

It was, however, only a respite. The problems which U Nu faced were horrifying. Burma had suffered appalling physical damage in the war; apart from bombing, the scorched earth tactics of retreating armies had resulted in the destruction of most of the extractive industries' plant and much of the communications by land and water. It took a long time for a socialist government, continually urged by its communist allies to expropriate all foreign enterprise without compensation yet lacking native resources of skill and experience to run them, to reach agreements for the re-opening of these industrial projects. Some of them have not yet regained anything like their pre-war efficiency. Those Indians who had remained in, or returned to, Burma lost their citizenship and most of their land; while the wrangles about compensation dragged on, their co-operation in reconstruction was small. Much of the rice bowl had reverted to jungle or been flooded by sea water.

Above all, there were the two problems of the minority races and of the lawless armed bands that had emerged from the chaos of war. Aung San's private army, now known as the People's Volunteer Organisation (PVO), had remained under arms, and a section of it (the 'White Band' PVO) collaborated in violence with the more extreme communists. During 1948 the whole of Burma erupted in rebellion, racial and political revolt adding to the chaos already caused by dacoity and the continued existence of independent armed bands. Civil government, restored at the insistence of the nationalists, had come too soon to permit the Allied military authorities to disarm the wartime irregular forces and collect the arms and ammunition left behind by the retreating Japanese.

In March, 1948 (the year in which communist rebellions took place all over South-east Asia), the communists revolted in Lower Burma. Sections of the Karens and Mons also rose, the White PVOs turned against the government, and a large part of the Army mutinied and joined one faction or another

87

of the rebels. In March, 1949, there was a violent Karen insurrection, and Karen forces took Mandalay and almost captured Rangoon. By July, 1949, U Nu's government still controlled Rangoon and the other seaports, but very little else; government forces were isolated in widely scattered pockets with their communications almost non-existent. Rice production and exports had fallen still further and the economic situation looked almost as hopeless as the military. Despite foreign aid and the assistance of a British military mission and war materials, it looked as if the newly independent country was dissolving into chaos.

It is difficult, in the light of his subsequent failures, to regard U Nu as a great leader. Nevertheless, this was his finest hour, and his courage and perseverance certainly earned the gratitude of Burmese posterity. Against all the odds, by a combination of political compromise and military action, the government managed not only to survive but gradually to win back territory that had passed out of its control. By the end of 1950 the situation had greatly improved, and in the middle of 1951 it became possible to hold a general election, at which U Nu and the AFPFL won a large majority. Backed by Colombo Plan and American technical aid, the government launched an ambitious series of social reforms and economic plans. Most of the PVO had been disbanded, and in 1952 a Karen state was created within the Union.

The position had improved from apparently hopeless to moderately hopeful. Nevertheless, nothing in Burma, since independence, has ever quite worked. The minority rebellions were never totally quelled; the frontier tribes were never entirely reconciled; law and order were never fully restored over the whole of a country in which dacoits and guerrillas could operate with comparative ease; to add to Burma's troubles, a large force of Chinese Kuomintang troops crossed the frontier after the communist victory in China and settled in the Shan mountain areas, raiding indiscriminately into Burma, Thailand and China.

Above all, the political compromises never quite succeeded

in producing any real political unity. Once the main objective of independence from the British had been achieved, and when the danger from anti-Burman revolts by minority races seemed to be passing, the Burman nationalists began to fall apart again. The whole political apparatus was marked by an amateurishness amounting to irresponsibility. Moreover, some of the compromises had been bought at a high price. It took years to agree upon terms for restarting the basic industries in collaboration with foreign companies, since the communists were violently opposed to the re-entry of the 'capitalists' on any terms at all. The communists then had to be bought off. In 1953 the government terminated the Economic Aid Agreement with the United States; in 1954 the defence agreement with Britain was ended and the military mission withdrawn.

Finally, the centrifugal forces inside the AFPFL itself grew too strong to be controlled. In 1956 a general election had given the League a reduced, but still large, majority. In April, 1958, the AFPFL split into two factions, the group opposing U Nu being led by two important members of the government. These were the Deputy Prime Minister Ba Swe, an astute politician and experienced labour leader, and the brilliant socialist intellectual Kyaw Nyein. U Nu, even with communist support, could count on a majority of only eight seats in the legislature.

The familiar troubles were piling up again. The economy was in bad shape, with chronic balance-of-payments crises; administration was inefficient, and the complicated controls and licensing arrangements had encouraged corruption; the secondary schools and colleges, instead of producing the educated and trained young people the country needed, were undisciplined stamping grounds for juvenile politicians. Burma was ripe for a military *coup*, since the Army seemed the only real focus for patriotism, honesty and efficiency. The transfer of power took place, however, without violence, for there was an Army leader who had earned the confidence of the politicians and was able to co-operate with them.

General Ne Win, Chief of Staff of the Army, had also been a Minister for many years. Of Sino-Burman parentage, and a former Thakin, he had borne the main burden of trying to restore some sort of order out of the chaos of rebellion and lawlessness, and had succeeded in virtually recreating a reliable Army. No government could have ruled without him, and he was therefore in a position to dictate his own terms. When he chose to do so, however, the terms were moderate and suggested none of the ambitions of a dictator. The assumption of power in Pakistan by Ayub Khan early in October, 1958, provided a precedent; Ayub Khan, however, remained in power. When Ne Win became Prime Minister of Burma on October 28, 1958, he proposed to remain in power for only six months. In the event it took him 18 months to clean up Burma, but in due course he relinquished office to the politicians.

Ne Win's main aim was to instil a sense of order, discipline and responsibility into a country which sorely needed them. He had some success. In certain fields, such as that of physically cleaning up Rangoon and other cities, he produced a real revolution which acted as a tonic to Burmese self-respect. Student indiscipline at Rangoon University and other colleges was quelled, and corruption was severely punished in the administration. With the assistance of Kyaw Nyein at the Ministry of Finance, the economic position began to improve. However, the lack of trained administrators and efficient managers in industry and commerce remained acute; Army officers had to take over more and more responsibilities.

Early in 1960 Ne Win redeemed his pledge and free elections were held in Burma. It is possible that the General would have liked the Ba Swe-Kyaw Nyein faction, now the main body of the AFPFL, to win. Certainly some of his senior officers made little secret of their own preference. Ne Win, however, remained strictly impartial, and even disciplined some of his officers who passed the limits of political neutrality. U Nu's Union Party won 161 out of 250 seats, and he became Prime Minister once more. The victory was in part due to U Nu's great personal popularity and prestige as the former associate and lieutenant of Aung San. It also owed something to his promise to introduce legislation making Buddhism the official state religion of Burma (some 85 per cent of the people being Buddhists), which gained him the strong support of the hierarchy and of the country's many monks.

It soon became clear that U Nu had lost his touch. He began to talk openly of entering a monastery; but his Union Party followers, knowing the extent to which their survival depended on his personal position, dissuaded him. He did his best to take the party strife out of politics, associating not only Ne Win but Ba Swe and Kyaw Nyein with as many as possible of the government's policies. When he went abroad, or travelled about Burma, one or more of the three generally went with him. With an eye to the future, however, Ba Swe managed to dissociate the AFPFL from any policies which appeared unpopular.

The promised State Religion Bill soon caused trouble. The original draft provoked strong protests from the minority religions, and when concessions were made the Buddhist hierarchy violently opposed the watering down of the Bill and charged U Nu with a breach of faith.

Racial rebellions began to menace the Union again. By the end of 1961 there were at least 3,000 Karen and Mon insurgents (and possibly many more), supported by militant communists, operating up to within 50 miles of Rangoon. In the Shan States to the east, guerrilla warfare against Shan rebels continued sporadically. In the extreme north, where large numbers of Chinese had been filtering illegally across the frontiers, a Kachin Independence Army was able to put 500 or more guerrillas in the field. There were also two communist groups. Since it has been proved everywhere in South-east Asia that it takes at least ten government soldiers to deal with one guerrilla in jungle or mountains, the Burmese Army was largely tied down in internal security duties. Moreover, U Nu was flirting with the idea of conceding more autonomous states.

The economic situation was again deterioriating rapidly. Ne Win's lieutenant, Brigadier Aung Gyi, was struggling to run not only the state Economic Development Corporation but also most of the former foreign trading companies, which had been nationalised by the simple expedient of starving them of import licences until the owners were only too anxious to sell them to the government cheap. Exports of rice and teak were still barely half the pre-war average, and mineral production had never recovered to anything like the pre-war level.

General Ne Win refrained from taking drastic action for a long time, and in the end he was probably driven to it as much by the urging of the Army officers as by his own patriotism. On March 2, 1962, a military *coup* removed the government, which was replaced by a Revolutionary Council under Ne Win's chairmanship. He retained in his own hands responsibility for defence, finance, national planning and law. U Nu was arrested, as were Ba Swe and other opposition leaders in the following year.

*　　*　　*

So the unhappy story of independent Burma culminated in the total collapse of democracy. It is not a story of which the Burmese can feel proud—nor can the British, who left the foundations of independent nationhood so ill-prepared. Army rule will probably hold the country together after a fashion: whether it can solve the fundamental problems is more doubtful. It will take years for the Karens, Shans and Kachins to settle down contentedly with the Burmans; until they do, the risk of disintegration is always present.

In fact, General Ne Win is far from having solved the minorities problem. He has not even succeeded in putting down insurgency, while being quite unprepared to make any concessions to separatist feelings. Believing profoundly that Burma must be held together firmly as a unitary state until its peoples begin to behave like a nation, he has actually reduced the degree of autonomy in the constituent states of the old Union of Burma.

In April, 1963, he offered a general amnesty to all the insurgents, and all the major groups except the Shans entered into negotiations with him. Only the non-communist Karen rebels concluded an agreement, the remainder holding out for a greater measure of autonomy than Ne Win was prepared to concede. Operations still continue.

Ne Win, like U Nu, is a socialist but not a communist. Indeed, in November, 1963, he carried out mass arrests of non-insurgent communists, at a time when he had not yet (as he did in 1964) banned political parties. It is true that he appointed two-Russian-oriented communists, Ba Nyein and Tin Mya, as his closest non-military advisers, but this was probably due to the difficulty of finding any competent coadjutors at all.

The task of trying to run a centralised socialist economy without experienced administrators and managers has proved Burma's biggest stumbling block since independence. More-over, the colonial trauma and the fetish of non-alignment have caused Burma to abjure the benefits of Western aid, so that she has of late years relied on reparations from Japan and some aid and credits from communist China. At the same time, the doctrinaire socialism practised by Ne Win has frightened off both foreign commerce and foreign investment. Overseas concerns, starting with the banks in 1963 and end-ing with the Burma Corporation and other concerns in 1965, have been taken over by the Government literally at the point of a gun.

Production has begun to increase, but Burma is a closed economy as well as a totalitarian state. Imports have been cut to the bone, and taxes are high.

The shadow of China looms large over Burma, which has cut herself off from any alliance or associations which could act as a counterbalancing factor. As a result, since U Nu's time, Burma has had to adopt a placatory attitude towards her giant neighbour, which has adopted a heavily paternal demeanour in return. The Sino-Burmese frontier has been demarcated and guaranteed, and state visits exchanged. There are those, however, in India as well as in Burma, who distrust China's ultimate intentions towards her neighbour. Chinese influence in the north of the country has certainly been increasing of late years, and any serious internal breakdown might well be followed by a communist takeover. This is now much more likely to occur as a result of internal minority insurgency than of economic collapse. General Ne Win and the Army, who alone stand between Burma and this fate, are unlikely to hand back power to politicians.

5
Indo-China and Thailand

THE present Kingdoms of Laos and Cambodia and the Republics of North and South Vietnam represent the territories of the former French Indo-China, bounded on the north by China, on the south and east by the South China Sea, and on the west by Burma, Thailand and the Gulf of Siam.

The area has been strongly influenced by both Hindu and Chinese cultures and contains a mixture of races from the north. The majority of the inhabitants are Buddhists, their religion being the last surviving legacy of Indian culture.

The first great civilisation of Indo-China was that of the Mon-Khmer racial group, whose capital can be seen in the splendid temple ruins of Angkor. Centred on the area of modern Cambodia, this great empire grew from about A.D. 800 to embrace much of what is now Laos, Vietnam and south-western Thailand. Despite a temporary defeat by the Chams at the end of the twelfth century, the Khmer empire survived until the invasion of Kublai Khan's Tartars opened the way for the continuous expansion of the Thais. The Khmers were forced back into the present region of Cambodia, where they remained squeezed between the Thais and the Annamites of Vietnam—for both of which races they still retain a hearty dislike and distrust.

The Thais, in addition to securing Siam and the temporary control of Burma (where they were called Shans), also settled in the north of what is now Laos, establishing rival principalities which have continued to dominate this little country. During the fourteenth century the three principalities of Luang Prabang, Xieng Khouang and Vieng Chan (now Vientiane) were united in the Kingdom of Lang Xang, which later won Champassak (now the southern province of Laos) from the Khmers and even conquered parts of Siam and Annam. It subsequently fell apart.

The Annamites, a Mongol race from central China, first settled in northern Vietnam some centuries before the Christian era. They were brought under the direct rule of China in the second century A.D.; they gained self-government in the tenth century, but remained under Chinese suzerainty until 1428. Thereafter they spread southwards down the coastal plain of Annam into Cochin China, whence they drove the Khmers in the eighteenth century. It was at this time that French influence first made itself felt in Indo-China, but by the end of the eighteenth century Vietnam was united under Annamite rule in the Empire of Annam.

The Annamites have throughout their history been deeply influenced by the Chinese, particularly in the north of Vietnam, where Taoism, the mandarin system and the patriarchal organisation of the family were well established.

In the middle of the nineteenth century the French gained their first lasting foothold in Indo-China by conquest. An expedition sent to avenge the death of a missionary in 1858 took Saigon. The whole of Cochin China (the southern extremity of Vietnam) was ceded to France as a colony. In 1863 the King of Cambodia saved his country from virtual extinction by the Thais by accepting French protection.

The Thais of Siam had always been of an expansionist disposition, ever ready to take advantage of their neighbours' troubles to snap up fresh territories on their borders. During the nineteenth century they also began to display considerable skill in playing off one European power against another. At the cost of some unpopularity with their neighbours, they succeeded in keeping their independence—the only country in South-east Asia that never became a European colony.

The British had started to trade with Siam as early as 1611, and the French made their first appearance there towards the end of the seventeenth century. Siamese expansion into the Malay states brought them into contact with the British there early in the eighteenth century, and the capture of Tennasserim in the first Anglo-Burmese war made some accommodation essential. It was, however, not until

1855 that a treaty was signed which gave Britain wide trading concessions and extra-territorial rights in Siam. Thereafter, while France was extending her conquests in Vietnam (both Annam and Tongking having become French protectorates by 1884), the British used the not unwilling Thais to check her expansion towards Burma and into China.

The Thais had already conquered the Kingdom of Vientiane, in Laos, in 1828, sacking the city of Vientiane; the Kingdom of Luang Prabang and the southern Laotian principality of Champassak became tributaries of Siam. In 1885, with British encouragement, the Thais had reached the borders of Vietnam, and the Emperor of Annam appealed to his French protectors for help. Thanks to the efforts of the French Vice-Consul Auguste Pavie, who succeeded in reconciling the rival Laotian rulers, the French were able in 1893 to take action against Siam. The British, having ascertained that the French aspirations were limited to Indo-China, advised the Thais to yield to France's ultimatum. The Kingdoms of Vientiane and Luang Prabang, together with the principality of Champassak, became the French protectorate of Laos.

This brought the British and French face to face. France having established herself on the Mekong River, the British crossed the upper Mekong from Burma, with the idea of establishing a Shan state to block French expansion towards China. Thanks to Pavie's diplomacy, however, an agreement was reached, and the French occupied the left bank of the Mekong as far as the northern frontier of modern Laos. France guaranteed the freedom of the Menam valley in Siam, but in 1907 succeeded in securing the retrocession to Cambodia of the provinces of Siem Reap and Battambang, which Siam had managed to acquire in 1863. The British renounced their extra-territorial rights in Siam by a treaty in 1909, Siam in turn renouncing her suzerainty over the northern Malay states.

A truncated Siam, shorn of her conquests, thus remained as an independent buffer state between British and French possessions. The Thais have not, however, forgotten their former glories, and have remained alert to retrieve anything that can be secured without undue risk. During the Second World War they took full advantage of the prevailing chaos in South-east Asia, but their triumph was short-lived.

★   ★   ★

The French impact on Indo-China was by no means uniform. Laos and Cambodia, acquired partly as buffer states between Siam and Vietnam and partly from a (quite erroneous) belief that the Mekong River could be made into a navigable highway for trade, were never economically exploited. Without through transport on the Mekong, they were never worth exploiting. The two protectorates remained, therefore, poor but nominally self-governing under French-educated rulers.

VIETNAM

Vietnam, however, was ready-made for exploitation, and the French dealt with it much as the British dealt with Burma. But whereas the British began by treating Burma as part of India, the French persisted in trying to make Vietnam a part of France. They made it enormously productive, and nearly all the profits went to France. As the British did in Burma, they came near to destroying the social structure of Vietnam without replacing it with a way of life satisfying to any but a small minority of westernised Annamites. As in Burma, the peasant standard of living scarcely rose at all. The French did at least try to control agricultural credit, and the Chinese in Vietnam never did quite as much harm as the Chettyars in Burma; but the peasants remained very poor.

In the over-populated north, holdings were normally too small for anything but the barest subsistence, and the money-lenders secured a strong hold on the peasants. In the south, where the French reclaimed large areas of swamp and jungle, they encouraged the opposite evil of over-large estates. The peasants grew their rice as share-cropping tenants of wealthy (and often rapacious) landlords, who also exploited them in the provision of usurious loans. The alternative was to work as coolies on French-owned rubber plantations.

Nevertheless, the French did transform Vietnam into an economically viable and potentially very rich country. They opened up communications, carried out admirable irrigation and flood-control works, and introduced a first-class medical service which greatly reduced endemic tropical diseases. The rice acreage, mostly in the Red River and Mekong deltas, increased fivefold and Vietnam became the world's third largest exporter (after Burma and Siam); coal production increased tenfold between 1900 and 1940, and rubber production rose from 200 tons to 76,000 tons in the thirty years before the Second World War. Saigon became not only a great and flourishing port but an attractive western metropolis, known as 'little Paris'.

Like most exploited peoples, however, the Annamites did not like it. As in Burma—and indeed everywhere in Southeast Asia—nationalist feeling in Vietnam began to become restive and articulate after the Russo-Japanese war; but there was an additional local stimulus in the revolutionary activities of Sun Yat-sen, who during his exile from China had his headquarters for a time in Hanoi. Only 25 years after the French began to colonise Vietnam, conspiracies against French rule were becoming common. During the 1920s there were frequent strikes and riots, culminating in a mutiny of Annamite levies in 1930. Left-wing governments in France introduced liberal reforms, but these could not affect the two fundamental causes of discontent, which were economic exploitation and the essentially assimilative, almost exclusively French system of administration. The French-educated *élite* were able to make little use of their education and talents, and the desire for independence grew.

* * *

What doomed French rule in Indo-China beyond hope of recovery, however, was the behaviour of the Vichy Government—and of the French colonists—during the Second World War.

The Japanese had had their eye on French Indo-China ever since they became involved in war on the mainland of Asia in 1931. It was the key to both southern China and the Malayan peninsula. (It is perhaps as well to remember that it still is, and that the Chinese know it as well as the Japanese did.) No French government between the wars had apparently concerted any strategy with Britain or the United States to deal with a Japanese threat to Indo-China, and France had maintained an attitude of dubious neutrality towards the conflict between Japan and China. When the war in Europe began, the Japanese put pressure on the French to cut off trade with southern China; when in February, 1940, the island of Hainan was occupied by Japan, the threat became obvious.

As soon as it became clear that France had been beaten in Europe, the Japanese moved in on Indo-China without opposition. There was no British fleet in the Far East, and the Americans had not yet made up their minds what to do. Japanese troops landed in Tongking before the end of 1940, the whole of Indo-China being occupied by the middle of 1941.

Meanwhile Siam saw the chance for which she had been waiting; at the beginning of 1941 she seized the Indo-Chinese provinces which the French had compelled her to disgorge. With Japanese approval, the Thais took back the Cambodian provinces of Siem Reap and Battambang, together with all Laos west of the Mekong River. Later, she was to resume the northern states of Malaya as well.

The Vichy Government and the French colonists in Vietnam collaborated with the Japanese, French administrators continuing to run the country under Japanese orders. This in itself was enough to lower, if not destroy, French prestige. But in addition the French themselves, so far from organising any resistance movement, took care to suppress any native Vietnamese resistance arising out of the nationalist movement.

And the nationalist movement was not the amateur business that it had been ten years before; it had found a leader who was ready and able to take advantage of the opportunities now available.

Nguyen Ai Quoc, now known to the world as Ho Chi Minh, was an experienced and well-trained communist organiser, He went to France as a boy before the First World War, and from Paris moved on in the early 1920s to Moscow, returning to his homeland via Canton, where he co-ordinated a plan of campaign with Borodin, the Russian adviser to Sun Yat-sen during the brief collaboration between the Comintern and the Kuomintang. Thereafter he engaged in underground activities for the party in various countries of South-east Asia, interrupted by two years' imprisonment in Hong Kong. By the time the war started Ho Chi Minh, working once more from China, had established the largely communist-directed Viet Minh (Viet Nam Independence League), which attracted the support of all militant Vietnamese nationalists and formed the main resistance movement of Indo-China under the Franco-Japanese rule.

The French, having lost the ultimate sanction of effective force, made no attempt to win the co-operation of the Vietnamese in common opposition to Japan. Even the possibility of French military co-operation with the Allies at the end of the war was forestalled by the Japanese, who in March, 1945, disarmed the French troops and arrested French officials. Prompted by the Japanese, the three native rulers—the Emperor Bao Dai of Annam, King Sisavang Vong of Luang Prabang in Laos and King Norodom Sihanouk of Cambodia —issued declarations of 'independence'. It was at least true that their countries were now independent of French rule, but they themselves were puppets of the Japanese. Ho Chi Minh refused to recognise Bao Dai's government, and the Viet Minh (ironically, in the light of subsequent events) actually received American military aid. It was able to free a part of northern Tongking from the Japanese before their general surrender to the Allies.

When that surrender came, there began the tragic and immensely complicated series of events which have made Laos and Vietnam the battleground of international power politics.

★   ★   ★

The Viet Minh declared Vietnam an independent republic, and set up a provisional government at Hanoi, in Tongking. It is as well to remind ourselves, in view of what has happened since, that the support received by Ho Chi Minh and the Viet Minh was limited neither to the Communists nor to the north of Vietnam. That Ho Chi Minh was, and is a communist does not alter the fact that the Viet Minh was at that time a nationwide and popular movement. It was able to take over power in Saigon with the obvious goodwill of the people of the south. The versatile Bao Dai promptly abdicated and lent his support to the new republican government. To all intents and purposes Vietnam was an independent and viable state. It may now seem a pity that it was not allowed to remain so.

But the French had no intention of relinquishing their claims to Indo-China, and General de Gaulle was the last man to allow France to be diminished in 1945. The Allies had agreed that France must be rebuilt as a European power, and all the other European allied powers were colonial powers. Whatever might happen to the Dutch, the British were already back in Burma and were preparing to reoccupy Malaya. The Potsdam Conference had accordingly decided that Indo-China should also be reoccupied: since the French were in no position to do this, it was agreed that it should be the responsibility of the British South-east Asia Command up to the 16th parallel, while China should occupy the northern areas of Laos and Vietnam.

The two allies discharged their obligations in typically different ways. The Chinese left the Viet Minh government firmly in control all the time they were in northern Vietnam, but refused to depart themselves until they had extracted a bargain from the French to their own advantage. The first British troops did not arrive in Saigon until the middle of

102

September; they found the Viet Minh in complete control, but General Gracey occupied key points in the city and released such French officials as had been imprisoned. Fearing for their safety, and for that of his own troops, since an agreement he had patched up between the French and the Viet Minh was breaking down, General Gracey occupied the whole of Saigon after some fighting and held it until enough French forces arrived to take over. This transfer took place in January, 1946, and in March the British withdrew entirely from Vietnam, having failed to achieve a compromise between the French and Vietnamese nationalists.

There is little doubt that a compromise could have been reached if the French had been at all willing. But they failed to recognise the strength of nationalist feeling and of the Viet Minh's position; in addition, they were obsessed with the fear that to yield in Indo-China would be to encourage nationalism in North Africa. In the event, they were driven from one concession to another, each made too late to bring about an accommodation with the Vietnamese. At first the French, while offering some degree of independence to what was in truth the *de facto* government of Tongking and Annam, tried to insist on retaining Cochin China as a separate entity on the grounds that it was a French colony rather than a protectorate like the northern territories. When this partition of the country was rejected by the Viet Minh, the French set up a puppet government in Cochin China. By the end of 1946 France and the Viet Minh were at war— a long, brutal, bloody war, which was to continue for nearly eight years.

The Viet Minh's struggle cannot be compared with the communist risings of 1948 in the other countries of Southeast Asia. For one thing it was not simply a communist rebellion: it was a genuine nationalist movement, aimed at independence from colonial rule and supported (at least in spirit) by the majority of the population. Secondly, the Viet Minh's initial military advantages were comparatively great. It virtually controlled the north of Vietnam, and had some guerrilla strength, outside the cities, in the south. Above all, it had arms. In addition to the American weapons made available to its resistance forces at the end of the war against Japan, it had been able to take possession of considerable quantities of Japanese, French and Chinese arms and ammunition after the Japanese collapse. With these, and some assistance from Soviet Russia, it was able to hold out against the French until the arrival of Chinese communist forces on the northern frontier of Vietnam made victory certain.

Not until 1949, when it was already too late, did the French take account of the political realities of the nationalist movement. Then, realising that it was no longer feasible to oppose the alternative of a French colonial régime to the Viet Minh's promise of a wholly independent Vietnam, they proposed that the country should enjoy the status of an Associated State in the French Union, and they set up what amounted to a puppet government under Bao Dai. But Bao Dai could not compare with Ho Chi Minh as the leader and symbol of a patriotic nationalist movement. Even when, after the victory of the communists in China, Ho Chi Minh abandoned his previous moderation and conditional offers of co-operation in favour of an uncompromising communist line, he still remained the focus of nationalist aspirations in Vietnam.

By 1953 the French were offering complete and total independence, with no reserved powers—but still within the French Union and without the right to secede from it. But by this time the war was lost. Dien Bien Phu fell in May, 1954, and on July 20 a cease-fire agreement was negotiated at the Geneva Conference. This left the Viet Minh in control of what is now the Democratic Republic of Vietnam, although it was emphasised that the ceasefire line on the 17th parallel was not to be regarded as a permanent line of partition.

It is no doubt true that after Dien Bien Phu the Viet Minh could have extended the area of its control well south of the 17th parallel. The great powers, however, were all in the mood for compromise. The French gift of realism belatedly reasserted itself; the British were content to settle for a communist frontier well north of Saigon and for neutral buffer states between Ho Chi Minh and Thailand; the Chinese were no doubt aware that the Americans had only narrowly been prevented from intervening directly in the war, and probably realised (with memories of what Japanese control of Saigon had meant) that the U.S. Government would certainly not tolerate a further advance southwards; the Americans, at the same time, did not want to become involved in an interminable mainland war with China; the Russians were content to call a halt at that point to Chinese-backed expansion.

The Geneva Conference thus divided French Indo-China into the component parts in which it remains today. The whole of Tongking and northern Annam, which included the Red River delta, Hanoi and the port of Haiphong, became the communist Democratic Republic of Vietnam (DRV); Southern Annam and Cochin China, including Saigon and the Mekong delta, remained temporarily under French military control, but became an independent state under Bao Dai. The Geneva agreement provided that free general elections should be held throughout the whole of north and south Vietnam, under international supervision in July, 1956, with a view to reunifying the country.

* * *

They were never held, because in 1956 the South Vietnamese simply did not trust the communists to hold free elections. Vietnam remained as firmly partitioned as Korea. In the north, the DRV developed as a more or less conventional communist state. Its population, even after the loss of about a million refugees to the southern state, has grown steadily and is now around 16·5 million people. It has scarcely managed to increase its rice production in proportion. Under the original Vietnam constitution of 1946 Ho Chi Minh remained President of the DRV, and no election was held to confirm him in office until 1960. He also held the Prime

Ministership until September, 1955, when he transferred this office to Pham Van Dong. But the next most important figures in the DRV, after Ho Chi Minh, were the pro-Chinese Truong Chinh and General Vo Nguyen Giap, once Foreign Minister and later Defence Minister and Commander-in-Chief of the Army. Giap was the victor of Dien Bien Phu, and has been the brain behind the Viet-Cong campaign in South Vietnam.

South Vietnam became constitutionally independent of the French, but at the time of partition Bao Dai was still technically Emperor. The effective leader of the south, however, was Ngo Dinh Diem, a Christian from a mandarin family with its roots in the north. In October, 1955, Diem (pronounced Zyem) held a referendum which produced an overwhelming majority in favour of the deposition of Bao Dai, who retired to France. Diem proclaimed South Vietnam a republic, of which he became President with American support and advice. He was re-elected in 1961, after a general election which the communists tried to sabotage and which was certainly not as free as it might have been—but which nevertheless probably did represent a reasonable vote of confidence in Diem.

Ho Chi Minh never abandoned his original purpose of uniting the whole of Vietnam under his own communist rule, and he and Giap laid their plans carefully. They did not make the Korean mistake of attempting a direct military invasion, which would have brought direct military intervention from the United States. It would also have been an open and undeniable violation of the Geneva agreement, and the International Control Commission (composed of India, Canada and Poland) which was set up by the Geneva signatories to ensure the cease-fire could not have failed to report the breach. This would not have suited the Russians, who as co-chairman of the Geneva Conference had undertaken responsibility for the settlement, although the Chinese might have been able to bear up under it.

In fact, the short land frontier between North and South

Vietnam has never been openly and demonstrably crossed by any formed body of armed communist troops—or at least the Control Commission has never been able to prove it. When the Viet Minh forces withdrew to the north of the 17th parallel, they took with them a considerable number of sympathisers from the south who were subsequently trained in the techniques of guerrilla warfare. An advance guard of agents and organisers was infiltrated into the south among the million refugees from the north. Large caches of arms were left in the northern provinces of South Vietnam. When the ground had been prepared by trained agitators travelling through the jungle from one village to another, terrorist activities were begun: at first small raids, then assassinations of government officials, village headmen and even provincial governors—all carefully planned to cause the maximum of alarm and to intimidate the rest. Finally, guerrilla activity started on a larger scale, both with men based in South Vietnam and with others infiltrated by sea and across the largely unpatrollable frontiers of Laos and even Cambodia.

By 1960 there were probably 12,000 armed Viet-Cong communist guerrillas in South Vietnam. At the end of 1961 there were at least 15,000. And in 1965 the Government claimed that there were as many as 64,000 'hard-core' guerrilla fighters, with perhaps another 100,000 or more in support. There were also at least 10,000 regular DRV troops engaged in mid-1965. Whether they will win is still uncertain, although it is quite certain that they would have won already had it not been for the military aid given by the United States. In 1962, President Kennedy committed the United States unmistakably to the defence of South Vietnam, and the Americans have since built up their fighting forces there to 75,000 men, to be increased to 125,000. Despite this, despite massive aid in arms and money, despite the assistance of experts trained in anti-guerrilla techniques in Malaya, despite the building up of government forces totalling around 500,000 men (including, in addition to the Army, the Civil Guard and village Self-Defence Corps), a considerable proportion of South Vietnam is under Viet-Cong control. The agricultural and industrial development of the country, which had been showing signs of progress, has been wrecked.

Arguments have raged interminably about the reasons for all this. There are still those who believe that Ho Chi Minh is rather a Vietnamese patriot than an international communist, that the peasants in the south are basically sympathetic to him, and that if he were allowed to reunite Vietnam it would become a peaceful and neutral country. If this were certain, all might be well. But is it really conceivable that Ho Chi Minh, a lifelong, Moscow-trained communist, would suddenly abandon communist techniques and ambitions in his relations with neighbouring countries? Even supposing that he is of the stuff of which Titos are made, he is growing old, and the Chinese are at hand to influence the choice and policies of his successor.*

Apart from the betrayal of promises made to those millions in the south who certainly do not wish to come under Viet-Minh rule—and it must be remembered that those who have remained loyal to their government and opposed the Viet-Cong would certainly suffer severely—could the West really take the risk of allowing South Vietnam to fall to the communists? The risk would be to Thailand, Cambodia, Laos and—ultimately—to Malaya. There are those who argue that communist China is not committed to an expansionist course; but if the argument proved to be wrong, it would be too late to halt the expansion. There are those who remember that Japanese occupation of South Vietnam was the basis of Japan's whole campaign and initial victories in Asia.

Finally, there were always plenty of people who maintained that President Diem's régime was a lost cause—that it had no basis of popular support and that the South Vietnamese would never fight for it with enthusiasm. This argument seemed to be proved right in 1963.

* Originally 'non-aligned' as between Moscow and Peking, Ho Chi Minh was persuaded by Truong Chinh to side with China in 1963. He may now be more amenable to Russian influence.

Diem himself was a remarkable, complicated and enigmatic character. He was a French-educated Roman Catholic, whose mandarin origins left a marked imprint on him. He and his brother Nhu evolved a somewhat baffling philosophy, a 'personalism' owing much to Maritain, but in which Chinese and even Buddhist elements were perceptible. Full of ideas and, at least in his early days of power, an energetic reformer with the ability to inspire enthusiasm and get things done, he was regarded as being personally incorruptible. Corruption and inefficiency were, however, certainly present lower down in his hierarchy, although both his Army and his civilian officials included a number of able and devoted men. A power complex, which stimulated both jealousy and scandal, developed around his family. His brother Nhu, possessed of an energetic and ambitious wife, was his most trusted adviser and Minister. Another of his brothers was Archbishop of Hue, probably responsible for much of the Buddhist hostility to the régime.

Diem's régime was the target of continuous abuse and hostile propaganda, not merely from the communists but from Asian neutralists and American liberals. The liberals argued that if the régime had been more 'democratic' and 'inspiring' communist successes would not have been so great. This is, to say the least, doubtful. It would almost be truer to say that if the Viet-Cong operations had not created such chaos in the country, the régime would have been much more successful and probably more democratic. It is in fact inconceivable that the situation could have been dealt with without severe emergency measures inconsistent with complete democratic freedom.

The criticism of President Diem, which certainly did the communists nothing but good, would perhaps have been more to the point if any of the critics had suggested earlier a convincing political alternative to the Diem régime. But many of the closest and best informed observers of the situation in South Vietnam believed that if the Viet-Cong could be destroyed at all—which was not by any means certain—the Western supporters of South Vietnam would probably have to try to save the country through the agency of the Diem régime.

The difficulty of finding a viable alternative to Diem was ironically emphasised by the manœuvres of the communists. Officially, the Hanoi government denied all connection with, and material support for, the Viet-Cong; it was a spontaneous 'liberation movement' organised and maintained wholly inside South Vietnam. In order, however, to make this appear really convincing it was necessary to give the movement an apparently indigenous and respectable leadership. Ho Chi Minh found it impossible to do this, and the attempts made have done little more than underline the basic problem. Apparently misled by an abortive *coup* against Diem in November, 1960, into believing that the régime was already ripe for supplanting, the communists formed at the end of 1960 a 'National Front for the Liberation of South Vietnam'. It embraced a wide variety of 'front' organisations, but it has not proved possible to put at its head any political figure of substance or popular appeal. The extent of the dearth of leaders may be gauged from the fact that there were even rumours that Hanoi was considering offering the puppet leadership to the adaptable Bao Dai. But in fact the NFLSV was merely a smoke-screen to hide the North Vietnamese communist direction of the Viet-Cong and to make imperialist invasion look like indigenous nationalism to gullible Western liberals.

Of these there are many. But the evidence of direction and armed support from Hanoi is overwhelming to anyone not blinded by prejudice—evidence from captured documents, from the International Control Commission (although in 1962 the Polish representative tried to have this evidence suppressed), even evidence from the speeches of Ho Chi Minh and other Hanoi leaders.

* * *

As the United States became more and more deeply involved in the South Vietnam operations, committing first aid and advisers, then air support and finally increasing numbers of American ground forces, their dissatisfaction with President Diem grew. This was a pity, for Diem was a genuine patriot and a valuable leader when properly handled. But by the end of 1961 Diem was beginning to wilt under the barrage of Western criticism and to lose his spirit for the fight. He withdrew progressively into isolation, and his arrogant and ambitious brother Nhu came more and more to the front. This was in every way a bad exchange, for he was opinionated, impossible to deal with, a ruthless secret police dictator, and lacked the respect and popularity which Diem had enjoyed (and earned) before it was undermined.

In 1963 the régime was on its last legs. More odium became attached to it when there was a flurry of Buddhist revolt, partly in genuine protest against Christian domination but largely organised as a political campaign. The unscrupulous organisers arranged a series of ceremonial public suicides of the most repulsive kind, in which wretched Buddhist monks burned themselves to cinders with petrol.

On November 1, 1963, an Army *coup* in Saigon overthrew the régime. Both Diem and Nhu were murdered, and a third brother, Ngo Dinh Can, tried and executed. There was an attempt both in South Vietnam and abroad to popularise the Army junta leader, General Duong Van Minh, and to glamourise him as the strong man who would win the war. But 'Big Minh' was not the man for the job, and in January, 1964, he was ousted by General Nguyen Khanh, who proved to be unpopular as well as incompetent.

To govern competently was in any case becoming increasingly difficult, since the fall of the Diem régime had been accompanied by the purging of nearly all the most honest and competent administrators. When Buddhist agitation boiled up again, Khanh resigned in August, withdrew his resignation and then faded quietly (but temporarily) from the scene, giving place to a Confucian civilian Prime Minister, Tran Van Huong. Mr Huong was honest, courageous and realistic, but the embattled Buddhists (assisted by communist agents) ousted him in his turn. Back came General Khanh, but after that confusion set in in earnest, and it soon became impossible to keep count of the succession of Generals and Air Marshals who flitted across the Saigon stage under the guise of 'governments'.

By the middle of 1965 the Americans—and indeed most of the South Vietnamese people—were bitterly regretting the heyday of President Diem (though not that of brother Nhu). For with the disintegration of government, the direction of the war against the Viet-Cong fell more and more on American shoulders. This lent colour to accusations of 'neo-imperialism' from the enemies of the United States, and made it more difficult to present American intervention as what it originally was and in truth still is—aid to an embattled ally under armed invasion. Some British socialists were already—though unsuccessfully—pressing the Prime Minister, Mr Harold Wilson, to withdraw support.

And the war was going badly. The Viet-Cong controlled two-thirds of South Vietnam—at least by night—and were meeting larger regular forces on equal terms and in pitched battles. Government forces were dispersed in often futile attempts to hold towns or 'strategic hamlets' against rebel units which seemed able to concentrate rapidly and at will.

Air attacks were begun on strategic objectives inside North Vietnam, and the United States announced its intention to build up its own forces in South Vietnam to no less than 125,000 men. Hanoi, confident of victory, refused to negotiate, rejecting all Harold Wilson's frantic efforts to pacify his left-wing supporters by mediating in Vietnam.

The United States Government, vilified abroad and criticised increasingly at home, set its teeth with admirable courage and settled down doggedly to a long war. And the courage involved was truly admirable, for it is not easy to persuade a comfortable people to send their sons to die thousands of miles away in a cause imperfectly understood and for a country that does not seem to amount to much anyway.

But indeed the cause is a good one, and the country is important. For if South Vietnam goes, then the whole of Indo-China must surely fall to communism, after which Thailand will be seriously at risk and Malaya threatened on two sides. It is easy to repeat the intellectuals' parrot-cry that this is a futile war which the West cannot win and which must soon be settled round the conference table. But the simpletons do not say how you attract to the conference table a communist country which is sure it can win by force of arms and disdains to negotiate—nor how, if you got it to the table, you could persuade it to concede anything at all.

The Americans are right; and Australia and New Zealand, two SEATO allies, endorsed this in 1965 by sending troops to Vietnam. If South Vietnam can be saved, it can only be saved by a long war which will convince the communists that they cannot win after all. Whether the American people have the patience and the determination to face this, only time will show. The danger of escalation, and Chinese intervention, is always present. But there is no easier way.

LAOS

Laos is a country nearly one-and-a-half times the size of South Vietnam but with less than one-fifth of its population. Much of it is mountainous or densely forested, and it is poor and undeveloped. Yet in the last eight years it has never been out of the newspaper headlines for very long and has been the subject of repeated conferences between the great powers involved in the cold war.

A glance at the map will suggest the reason for this. Laos is a landlocked country having frontiers with six other states, those with China, Burma and Cambodia being short but by no means unimportant. It is, however, the two long frontiers that are of particular significance. One is with both North and South Vietnam; the significance of this lies in the fact that a Laos with a government that is either sympathetic to communism or incapable of policing its frontiers can be used as a means of transit for communist guerrillas and supplies from the DRV to the Viet-Cong rebels in South Vietnam. The other long frontier is with Thailand, a member of SEATO and a country hyper-sensitive to any threat of communist invasion.

After the collapse of the Japanese the British occupying forces were able to hand over southern Laos to the French in reasonably good order. In the north, however, the Chinese forces occupying the territory north of the 16th parallel under the Potsdam agreement established an independent nationalist government at Vientiane. This was led by Prince Petsarath and formed largely by an independence movement called the Lao-Issarak. After the withdrawal of the Chinese at the beginning of 1946, French and Laotian royalist troops succeeded in defeating the Lao-Issarak forces. Vientiane was captured on April 24, and the revolutionary government fled to Thailand.

Under an agreement signed on August 27, the ancient kingdoms of Laos were reunited. The two kingdoms of Vientiane and Luang Prabang, including also the former Kingdom of Xieng Khouang, had already been united; now Prince Boun Oum, the feudal ruler of the southern part of Laos, formally renounced his hereditary rights to the throne of Champassak, which was incorporated in a single Kingdom of Laos under King Sisavang Vong of Luang Prabang. Luang Prabang remained the royal capital, but the administrative capital was fixed at Vientiane. Later in the year, as a result of French and American pressure, Thailand returned the Laotian provinces annexed in 1941.

Laos moved gradually towards complete independence. Internal self-government came with the promulgation of a new constitution for the Kingdom in May, 1947. On July 19, 1949, a treaty gave Laos the status of an independent state within the French Union. The Lao-Issarak was dissolved, and the majority of its members returned to the country from exile.

It was not to be expected that the war in Vietnam between

the French and Ho Chi Minh's communists would leave untouched a Laos which had both a long frontier with Vietnam and an energetic Annamite minority. Twice during 1953 Laos was invaded by Viet Minh forces, aided by a Laotian communist movement known as Pathet Lao, which contained a number of the communist members of the old Lao-Issarak and was led by Prince Souphanouvong, a member of a cadet branch of the Laotian royal family. After the second invasion, in December, 1953, fighting continued until the cease-fire arranged at the Geneva Conference in July, 1954. The agreement, which was to be supervised by the International Control Commission (India, Canada and Poland), provided among other things for the withdrawal of Viet Minh troops and of French troops other than members of a small military mission to train the Royal Laotian Army, and for the temporary concentration of Pathet Lao forces in the north-eastern provinces of Phong-Saly and Sam Neua.

A political settlement proved much harder to achieve—and indeed it has not been achieved yet. It was not until the end of 1957 that the neutralist Laotian government of Prince Souvanna Phouma reached and signed an agreement with Prince Souphanouvong and the Pathet Lao. This provided for the integration of the Pathet Lao armed forces into the Royal Laotian Army and reserves; the extension of central government control to the two provinces occupied by the Pathet Lao; the transformation of the Pathet Lao into a regular political party, which became known as the Neo Lao Hak Sat (Laotian Patriotic Front); and the admission of Prince Souphanouvong (Souvanna Phouma's half-brother) and one of his colleagues into the government.

Elections in the following year brought about a re-alignment of political forces, and a government representing a coalition of the Nationalist and Progressive parties (with the title of the Laotian People's Rally) was formed under Phoui Sananikone and Katay Sasorith. It soon became obvious that there were strong forces at work to prevent the success of a neutralist government, particularly one which rested on any sort of agreement with the communists. The Pathet Lao forces remained active, and there was sporadic fighting with government troops.

By the middle of 1960 there was considerable discontent in the country, the right-wing government having become notorious for the amount of corruption which flourished in its shadow (particularly in connection with the extensive opium trade). On August 9, 1960, the government was ousted by a military *coup*. A patriotic young Army officer, Captain Kong Lae, took over Vientiane in a single smooth operation with one parachute regiment. Perhaps unfortunately for the future history of Laos, he had no very clear idea what to do with it once he had taken it. In the event, the immediate successor to office was again Prince Souvanna Phouma, who once more sought to establish a neutralist coalition. He was promptly opposed by General Phoumi Nosavan, who now emerged as the would-be strong man of Laos. An ambitious politician, as well as a soldier, Phoumi no doubt intended to emulate Ne Win of Burma; he set up a Revolutionary Committee with headquarters at Savannakhet in the south, where the feudal ascendancy of Prince Boun Oum was sufficiently impressive to cause Phoumi to instal him as leader.

In addition to Kong Lae's own regiment, other units of the Royal Laotian Army remained loyal to Souvanna Phouma, and these were later swelled by civilian recruitment. But General Phoumi's forces were strong enough to recapture Vientiane in December, 1960. The Souvanna government had already been declared illegal by King Savang Vatthana (who had succeeded to the throne in 1959), and Souvanna himself had fled to Phnom Penh in Cambodia. Enough of the National Assembly to give an appearance of legality to the formation of a new government was persuaded to meet at Savannakhet, and Prince Boun Oum became Prime Minister, with General Phoumi Nosavan as Deputy Premier.

Civil war, aided by foreign intervention on both sides, was now almost inevitable, for the Western powers recognised the Boun Oum government while the communist and some neutralist countries continued to recognise Souvanna Phouma as Prime Minister. Despite efforts, especially by India and by Prince Norodom Sihanouk of Cambodia, to reconvene the International Control Commission and to hold a conference of interested powers, the split grew steadily worse.

For this, as for the greater part of the tragedy of Laos, the Western allies—and in particular the United States—must be held chiefly to blame. In 1957, despite French attempts to secure support for Souvanna, the influence of the U.S. Secretary of State, Dulles, had persuaded the SEATO powers into distrust of the prospects for a neutralist government dependent on agreement with communists. It was then that the best chance of securing a stable and peaceful Laos, forming with Cambodia a neutral buffer between both Vietnam and Thailand, was lost. A second chance came with Souvanna's return to power after the Kong Lae coup in 1960. By that time Britain had come round to the French view and was willing to seek a neutralist solution; but the Americans and the Thais remained adamantly opposed to Souvanna and insisted on providing General Phoumi with advisers and military aid. By sheer bad luck, this chance came during the last weeks of the Eisenhower Administration; by the time the new Kennedy Administration had reassessed the situation, Souvanna had been driven into the arms of the communist Pathet Lao.

Kong Lae's troops and the Pathet Lao joined forces on the strategically important upland Plaine des Jarres. On December 30 they captured a vital airfield there near Khang Khay, and before long a regular airlift of supplies and war materials had been established by Russian aircraft staging from Hanoi in North Vietnam. On January 31, 1961, Prince Souvanna Phouma's government was formally reconstituted at Xieng Khouang; prominent in it was Quinim Pholsena, formerly left-wing leader of the Peace Party. Souvanna left shortly on a world tour to secure support for his policies, but was unable to secure a hearing in Washington.

Meanwhile, the Kong Lae-Pathet Lao forces secured a firm grip on much of northern and eastern Laos, opening safe communications with China and North Vietnam and gaining a number of important strategic positions. Much of this success was gained through skilful small-scale guerrilla operations, to which General Phoumi's forces and their American advisers (like the French before them) had no effective counter-tactics at all; the Pathet Lao, on the other hand, could draw on the skill and experience of North Vietnamese experts. In addition, it soon became clear that in any major operation Phoumi's troops were for the most part unreliable.

It was already obvious that the American decision to underwrite Phoumi was a major error, if only because he was simply unable to win. The basic assumption that a neutralist government relying on co-operation with communists must in the end lead to communist domination of Laos—a view which Phoumi and many Americans have always strongly maintained—may have been (and may yet be proved) right: but it had been even more certainly proved by April, 1961, that a right-wing government aligned with the West was simply not viable in Laos. The taint of past corruption and incompetence was too strong, and neither Boun Oum nor Phoumi was capable of inspiring nationalist feeling and attracting effective support among either the peasants or the educated young people of the towns.

The great powers now got together to hammer out a solution, somewhat hampered by the fact that East and West recognised different Laotian governments. But by the end of April, Britain and Russia had agreed to call for a cease-fire, and at the beginning of May the Control Commission returned to Laos. The cease-fire appeared to come just about in time to save Phoumi's forces from complete defeat. A prolonged and frustrating period of horse-trading followed at two political levels. The usual 14-power conference argued on the usual cold-war basis at Geneva; meanwhile the 'Three Princes'—Souvanna Phouma, Boun Oum and the communist

Souphanouvong—parleyed rather in the manner of rival barons in the Wars of the Roses.

The negotiations dragged on for more than a year, during which time both the United States and the communist powers tried to build up the strength of their respective champions in Laos.

There seemed to be some confusion in the policies of the various United States government departments: while President Kennedy and the Secretary of State appeared to share the view held by the British and French (and now also by Australia) that a neutralist coalition under Souvanna Phouma offered the best hope of a settlement, some American officials in Vientiane still appeared to be encouraging General Phoumi to hope for a right-wing victory. Phoumi needed little encouragement, and even at the end of 1961 was still talking openly of a choice between 'a communist Laos and war'. This, moreover, was after the three Princes had agreed in June to form a coalition government, and had in October agreed in principle that the King should appoint Souvanna Phouma as Prime Minister with a Cabinet to consist of eight neutralists, four followers of Boun Oum and four Pathet Lao representatives. Boun Oum, urged on by Phoumi, insisted that the key portfolios of Defence and the Interior should be given to his group; this was of course quite unacceptable to the Pathet Lao, and Souvanna Phouma not unreasonably determined that they must be in the hands of his own centre group rather than given to either right-wing or communist ministers.

For several months Boun Oum and Phoumi refused even to send delegates to treat with the other side in Laos, on the pretext that their safety could not be guaranteed in territory held by the Pathet Lao. When finally meetings were arranged, no agreement was reached; meanwhile, Boun Oum and Souvanna Phouma each claimed to be *de jure* Prime Minister. Finally it became clear that the precarious military situation in Laos was deteriorating again into civil war, and the United States applied extreme pressure by suspending economic aid to Laos. Even then General Phoumi remained obdurate, and in March, 1962, Mr Averell Harriman was unable in a personal interview to persuade him to enter the coalition. In May, Phoumi and Boun Oum undertook a tour of right-wing Asian governments in a desperate attempt to rally some support; Quinim Pholsena and Kong Lae simultaneously visited Moscow and Peking. In the absence of these leaders, the Pathet Lao suddenly launched a major attack on the north-western centre of Nam Tha and won a considerable victory over the ineffective right-wing forces.

This marked the end of everybody's patience, and even Phoumi had to admit that the game was—at least temporarily —up. The three Princes reached agreement, on Souvanna's terms, signed it on June 12 and had it approved by the King on June 23. The Geneva Conference was at last able to adjourn, having agreed the new Laotian Government's declaration of neutrality and committed everything to writing.

Thus, after nearly five years of war and progressive economic deterioration, the solution that had been possible in 1957 was finally accepted in 1962. American unwillingness to relinquish the dream of a Western-aligned Laos may yet prove to have brought about the worst American nightmare —a Laos under communist domination. For the situation had deteriorated very markedly in those five years.

In 1957 Prince Souvanna Phouma was at the height of his influence, unsoured by disappointment and almost certainly with the ability and authority to control the Pathet Lao; General Phoumi Nosavan had not yet been seized by delusions of grandeur; and above all the Pathet Lao did not control half the country. In 1962 the Pathet Lao had won a decisive military victory and was at the summit of its prestige; it looked very much as if the influence of Prince Souphanouvong would in any crisis outweigh that of Souvanna and Kong Lae.

In addition, the Pathet Lao victory over General Phoumi had enabled the communist powers to win a number of concessions in international negotiations. After 1962, the influence of the International Control Commission in Laos was much diminished, and the West had virtually no means of ensuring that the communists carried out their obligations. The 1962 agreement did not provide for the disarmament of either side, and there was grave doubt whether the DRV forces—which everyone except the DRV acknowledged to have been operating in Laos—were being withdrawn in accordance with the agreement. In fact, unlike the Americans, they were not withdrawn. They are still there, in control of the Pathet Lao.

General Phoumi, together with the Thais and (until 1961) the Americans, had maintained all along that a neutralist government which included Pathet Lao elements was bound in the end to fall completely under communist domination. Whereas this was probably not true in 1957, or even 1960, it may well have been true by 1962, when it was too late to do anything about it. Souvanna Phouma's new government certainly made a great business of being neutral: under the influence of its extreme wings, it recognised both régimes in Vietnam and Germany and also both the Peking and Taipeh governments. It officially contracted out of all alliances and entanglements and announced that it did not wish to be protected by SEATO under the terms of the protocol to the Manila Treaty.

Was it conceivable that Souvanna could hold his team together, and that Phoumi and Souphanouvong could collaborate indefinitely? It was not. It was also doubtful whether the Pathet Lao, backed by the DRV, would allow the transit route for Viet-Cong supplies from North to South Vietnam to be closed. There remained also the risk that Thailand's allies in SEATO might not be able to prevent the Thais from taking some rash action if the communist threat to their frontiers seemed acute, although the specific United States guarantee to Thailand helped to prevent this.

Early in 1963 there was a series of political assassinations of neutralists, culminating in the murder of the Foreign Minister, Quinim Pholsena. Kong Lae, already alarmed by the increasing infiltration of North Vietnamese forces and their domination of the Pathet Lao, fell out with the communists and was deserted by his lieutenant, Colonel Deuane Sipaseuth. Kong Lae and General Phoumi, those ancient enemies, formed an alliance of despair.

Before long the coalition had clearly broken down. Prince Souphanouvong and another Pathet Lao minister, Phoumi Vongvichit, left Vientiane for Pathet Lao territory. Attempts at a rapprochement failed, as did appeals from the British and Russian co-chairmen of the Geneva Conference. Finally, in April, 1964, the remains of the coalition Government were overthrown by a right-wing *coup* led by General Kouprasith Abhay and a junta of Army officers which for once did not include General Phoumi Nosavan. Although the now almost wholly disillusioned Prince Souvanna Phouma was reinstated as premier, Vientiane was now controlled by the military.

But in fact Laos was effectively partitioned, with the communist Pathet Lao—controlled by North Vietnamese—in command of much of the country. The indefatigable Kong Lae took the field again and was soundly beaten by the Pathet Lao forces. Chaos had come again to Laos, and this time the Russians were unresponsive to British calls for a joint approach to sort out the mess. The Kosygin line was different from Khrushchev's.

Yet the prospect of a stable neutral Laos, forming with Cambodia a buffer between North Vietnam and Thailand, is —and has always been—so desirable that it is worth much to the West to help make it a reality. It may also, in the light of present differences between China and Soviet Russia, possibly be in Russia's interests too. Whatever the fate of governments, there is a real desire on the part of the overwhelming majority of Laotians to be, and to remain, genuinely neutral in the Asian cold war; in this they are at one with the Cambodians. It may be that this desire will in the end prevail over the ambitions and jealousies of political factions and over communist aims. Above all, Laos now needs a period of peace and reconstruction, together with large quantities of economic aid, for she is not viable by herself. Here again, if Russia and the West, together with neutral powers, could agree to offer genuine and disinterested help, the effort of reconstruction might cement Laos together for good.

CAMBODIA

In Cambodia, where the nationalist movement had always been weaker than in Vietnam, independence from France had been achieved with little bloodshed. The old racial antipathy and national rivalries which separated the Khmers from both Annamites and Laos helped to keep the people of Cambodia apart from the main stream of Indo-Chinese nationalism. The Viet Minh did their best to secure control of Cambodia, but they—and the French—were outmanœuvred by the young King Norodom Sihanouk. The Cambodian nationalists had been led by Son Ngoc Thanh, a collaborator of the Japanese and puppet Prime Minister at the end of the war. With the King's approval, Thanh was arrested by the British and removed to detention in France. This left the way clear for the King to become the leader and symbol of a truly Cambodian nationalist movement, and he allowed no competitors to stand in his path.

Gradually, with that mixture of shrewdness, blackmail, bluff and flamboyantly dramatic courage that has become his hallmark, he extracted the necessary concessions from the French to make Cambodia genuinely independent. Meanwhile, the French had persuaded Thailand to disgorge the long-disputed Cambodian provinces of Siem Reap and Battambang.

When Son Ngoc Thanh returned from exile, the King refused to co-operate with him; Thanh took up arms with the nationalist Khmer Issarak guerrillas, in alliance with communist Viet Minh bands drawn from the Annamite minority in Cambodia. The King promptly dismissed his inept government, took emergency powers into his own hands, and by the end of 1953 had won the substance of independence from the French.

His dominance, however, suited neither Thanh nor the communists, and in the following year regular Viet Minh forces invaded Cambodia from Vietnam. Not only did the Cambodian royal forces prevent the invasion from succeeding, but the King held out at the Geneva conference for the complete removal of the Viet Minh from his country. Despite communist efforts to retain a foothold in Cambodia, the King won his point; the Viet Minh had to withdraw, Son Ngoc Thanh's attempts to reinstate himself were rebuffed, and the Khmer Issarak guerrillas were forced to surrender.

The King was now a national hero, and he determined to use his enormous prestige to the best advantage. Impatient with the intrigues and obstruction of the politicians, he actually did what Bernard Shaw's King Magnus threatened to do in *The Apple Cart*. On March 3, 1955, he abdicated in favour of his parents (the Cambodian monarchy being—at least in theory—elective, he had himself succeeded a King who was both his cousin and his grandfather); he then formed his own political party, swept the country with a flame of passionate oratory and a shrewd talent for fixing things, and won all the seats in the National Assembly at the general election in September.

Prince Norodom Sihanouk, as he now is, thus became his country's Prime Minister and virtual dictator—although his popularity is such that he has never needed to employ the methods of dictatorship. In 1960 his father died, and a council of regency was appointed. With his peculiar talent for having things both ways, Sihanouk had his mother the Queen-Dowager named 'Symbol of the Throne' and himself assumed the self-created office of Head of the State. He has continued to rule Cambodia in a wholly charismatic aura, almost literally worshipped by his people, surrounded with fawning adulation from an almost unbelievably servile press and radio, and addressed by diplomats with the high-sounding title of 'Monseigneur'.

So far, despite a temperament that occasionally appears to be about to swamp his natural calculating shrewdness (and he has been called everything from a playboy to a paranoiac by his enemies), he has done well for his country. He has retained the goodwill of the French and at one time secured a great deal of American economic aid. Sticking firmly to an unswerving neutralist line, he has also received aid from Russia, China and other communist countries.

Cambodia is still a poor country. About half of its 70,000 square miles is jungle and forest, and the remainder contains only 5 million people, mostly rice-growers in the river valleys, Yet it is being gradually developed. It is terribly short of educated and competent administrators, but foreign technical aid has been quite effectively used, with less waste and corruption than is common in South-east Asia. Crops are being diversified and agricultural methods improved; a few industries have been started; and communications are being developed, with a new deep-water port on the Gulf of Siam (named, typically, Sihanoukville) connected with the capital, Phnom Penh, by a modern highway and a railway under construction.

Until now, Sihanouk's unyielding and somewhat self-righteous neutralism has paid dividends, and there are few who would maintain that Cambodia would have been better off today if she had become embrangled in the cold war manœuvres that have brought Laos and South Vietnam to their present sorry state. However, in the light of Sihanouk's high-minded admonitions to his occasionally exasperated neighbours, it is perhaps worth while to examine Cambodia's position a little more closely. It is, indeed, something of a test case for neutralism.

The first thing to strike one, of course, is that Cambodia has not hitherto had a frontier with a communist country; and this, to put it no higher, does make it easier to remain successfully neutral in the cold war. There has certainly been some communist infiltration across Cambodian frontiers, which are in places impossible to police, but this has been largely transit traffic connected with the guerrilla war in South Vietnam rather than aimed at Cambodia itself. If Laos falls completely under communist control, and if the Viet-Cong campaign in South Vietnam were to continue successfully for much longer, the position of Cambodia would become much more difficult.

The best long-term solution in Indo-China is almost certainly a genuinely neutral buffer between Thailand and Vietnam, consisting of a Laos and Cambodia that are both politically stable and economically viable. Whether this is possible for Laos is doubtful. It is certainly possible for Cambodia, but it is hard to feel sure that even Sihanouk can maintain his position in isolation. If South Vietnam, as well as Laos, were to fall to the communists, infiltration of Cambodia would probably follow, and it is doubtful whether the Thais would allow this to proceed unchecked.

Meanwhile, the Khmers' traditional fear and distrust of the Thais and the Vietnamese were matched by a strong personal and political antipathy between Sihanouk on the one hand and Field-Marshal Sarit Thanarat, Prime Minister of Thailand, and President Ngo Dinh Diem of South Vietnam on the other. To Diem, engaged in a war against communist guerrillas organised from North Vietnam, and to Sarit, menaced by the south-westward pressure of communism, a neutralist in Indo-China seemed more like a traitor than a buffer. Diem openly accused Sihanouk (almost certainly mistakenly) of deliberately giving aid and comfort to Viet-Cong bands who used eastern Cambodia as a base for operations in Vietnam. And Sarit insulted Sihanouk in 1961 in a speech so offensive that Sihanouk flew into a passion and broke off diplomatic relations with Thailand, closing the frontier, mobilising his army and threatening to call in the Chinese to help him. All of which was no doubt carefully calculated, but did nothing to change Sarit's expressed opinion that Sihanouk was a hysterical nuisance. It also seriously interfered with the valuable tourist traffic to Angkor Wat.

The deaths of Diem and Sarit did little to mollify the Prince's dislike of Annamites and Thais, and he continued on his flamboyant and successful way, with a few excursions to international neutralist rallies. In 1963, after a visit to Peking and New Delhi, he put on a splendid show to quell some local dissatisfactions, threatening to dissolve his party and return to private life; to make it more convincing, he offered his job to any of his critics who would take it. None accepted, and he was implored to stay at the helm. This he did.

In 1963–64, the hotting up of the South Vietnam war and the increasing American military activity there led to some serious frontier clashes with Cambodia and to the breaking off at one time of diplomatic relations with the U.S. and Britain. Viet-Cong guerrillas crossing the frontier were pursued, and Cambodia claimed an infringement of her neutrality. The fact that this neutrality was being regularly infringed by the Viet-Cong in the unpoliceable jungle was ignored by Prince Sihanouk, who was more justifiably enraged when American and South Vietnamese forces accidentally attacked a Cambodian village. Cambodian forces began to fire across the frontier and even to cross it themselves.

For a time Cambodia and South Vietnam seemed on the brink of war; but this was not at all Prince Sihanouk's line. After some fiery speeches in which he called for American withdrawal from Asia and threatened to call in the Chinese, he relented—and even graciously offered to accept some American economic aid again. Nevertheless, for all Sihanouk's by-play, Cambodia is at risk, and the Prince is seriously concerned for his neutrality. It ought to be guaranteed.

THAILAND

It remains to bring up to date the story of Thailand, the name adopted by the Kingdom of Siam in 1949.

Siam had been ruled by an absolute monarchy ever since King Uthong established the first capital at Ayudhya in 1350—when Bangkok was still a range of mud banks in the sea. King Rama I, founder of the present royal dynasty in 1782, also founded Bangkok, and his descendants ruled there with at least the appearance of despotic power until 1932, when a gentlemanly and slightly apologetic *coup d'état* by middle-class officers and officials produced a new constitution which substituted a political oligarchy for absolute monarchy. There was a certain façade of democracy provided, and there have been elections in Thailand, but the normal method of changing the government since 1932 has been by *coup d'état*. For 25 years politics involved little more than a struggle for power between two of the leaders of the 1932 revolutionary party, one a civilian and the other a soldier.

The former, Pridi Banomyong, was an intellectual left-wing nationalist. The man who was to become Field-Marshal Pibul (or Phibun) Songgram was an ambitious and astute politician. During the war Pibul was Prime Minister and collaborated with the Japanese, while Pridi secretly organised resistance to them. Pibul dutifully declared war on the Allies, but the United States decided to ignore this and subsequently treated Thailand as an occupied friendly country. (Britain, however, found it convenient to recognise the declaration of war, in order to enforce a peace treaty afterwards on favourable terms. It should be remembered that Thailand had during the war annexed the Shan States of Burma and the four northern states of Malaya, as well as provinces of Laos and Cambodia, which was felt to have been an unfriendly act. However, it was all settled quite amicably, with that ready acceptance of the inevitable which is as characteristic of the Thais as their readiness to snatch an advantage.) As the end of the war drew near, Pibul gracefully withdrew into temporary retirement, and Pridi finally became Prime Minister in March, 1946.

Pibul, however, was by no means finished, nor could Pridi establish his position. In June, King Ananda Mahidol was found dead with a bullet wound in his head. He may well have committed suicide, but an accusation of murder (and, of course, it might have been a murder) was a useful political weapon. Pridi was forced to resign, and at the end of 1947 fled the country after a *coup d'état* restored Pibul to power.

Pridi never recovered, and Pibul became virtually dictator of Thailand, to the considerable profit of himself and a circle of his associates, including General Phao Siyanon, the Chief of Police. He was finally ousted by his Minister of Defence, who was also Commander-in-Chief of the Army (as well as being involved in some profitable commercial ventures). General (later Field-Marshal) Sarit Thanarat organised the usual *coup d'état* in 1957, and both Pibul and Phao left Thailand. After an interim government under Pote Sarasin (later Secretary General of SEATO), Sarit put up General Thanom Kittikachorn as Prime Minister. Whether this was ever intended to be more than a temporary interlude is doubtful; Thanom, an honest and respected soldier, was not a great public figure, and before long he became deputy-premier and yielded the appearance of power to Sarit, who already held the substance.

The history of the Thais has been sufficiently peculiar to make anyone chary of prophecy concerning their future. The internal situation is perhaps easier in some ways to analyse than the country's future position in the world. Economic progress, under the Sarit régime and since, has been by no means negligible. Bangkok, a large and (in parts) glittering Westernised capital city, shows many of the signs of the Affluent Society, and has certainly absorbed an excessive proportion of the foreign aid and capital put into the country. But the situation in the countryside is markedly better than in most of the countries of South-east Asia, largely because there is a genuinely independent peasant agriculture and little population pressure on the land. Something like 85 per cent of Thailand's 31 million people work on the land, and nearly 90 per cent of all agricultural land is farmed by its owners. There is little under-nourishment by Asian standards. The currency is sound and stable, and exports of rice and rubber remain high.

Diversification of agriculture has been encouraged, and the setting up of industries—mostly with foreign capital—has proceeded steadily and with some success. The national income has been expanding fairly regularly at a rate of 4 to 5 per cent a year. The government is sensitive to any signs of local economic distress—particularly in the eastern provinces on the Laotian frontier, where special efforts have been made to prevent discontent by pressing on with economic aid and development. After a long campaign to break the former commercial stranglehold of the large Chinese minority and to stop further Chinese immigration, a real effort has been made to assimilate the resident Chinese and to reach an acceptable *modus vivendi* with them.

All this meant that the right conditions did not appear to be present in Thailand for internal communist subversion to be successful. Yet a country so subject to military *coups d'état* can hardly be called politically stable. From the practical point of view, of course, its political—and, as a result, its economic—stability has been and is much greater than that of Burma or Indonesia, for example. When Sarit died in December, 1963, it was reassuring to find that stability did not depend entirely on one man. He was succeeded without argument or unrest by the deputy-premier, General Thanom Kittikachorn. It appeared that Thailand was maturing.

It is important to understand in what sense Thailand is a military dictatorship. Although political opposition to the régime is virtually impossible, Thailand is not a total police state in the way that Afghanistan is. There is certainly far more personal freedom than in any communist state. Nor is the country run, in detail, by the Army in the way that Burma (and in many respects Indonesia) is. Sarit's and Thanom's cabinet contained a number of civilian Ministers who ran their own departments and to whose advice they listened. Nevertheless, the basis of the régime's power and authority was originally, and presumably still is, the control of the Army.

There have never been effective democratic institutions in Thailand; nor have there ever been any popularly based political parties, as distinct from factions attached to individual contenders for power. This can perhaps be attributed to two causes: first, the absence of any exploitable peasant unrest; and second, the fact that the concentration of commercial activities in the hands of the Chinese has prevented the rise of any effective Thai middle class, apart from Army officers and officials. For political parties to flourish, there have to be interests to support them and be represented by them. This situation will certainly arise in Thailand sooner or later, but until it does there is no effective counter-check to the power of the Army officers.

It is impossible to say when a durable constitution will emerge in Thailand. At present there does not seem to be the political interest or talent available to make one work. It is probably not quite out of the question that the Thanom régime might one day be succeeded by a government with a preponderant civilian element. If it is, the Foreign Minister, the part-Chinese Thanat Khoman, might well play a leading part in it; but it would probably have to be headed, at least for a time, by a respected military figure. On past form, however, it is still possible—though less likely—that there will be another military *coup*.

To what extent any change of régime would be likely to alter Thailand's foreign policy it is hard to say, but probably such a change would not of itself have much effect. This is not to say that Thailand's alignment may not change, even under so strong an anti-communist as General Thanom. In the last resort, for all their present fervent alignment with the West in SEATO, the Thais are certainly no more deeply concerned than any other country in South-east Asia with anyone's interests but their own.

Relations between Thailand and Tunku Abdul Rahman's Malaysia are good, perhaps despite—rather than because of

—the existence of a substantial Malay minority in southern Thailand. Although Malaysia is not a member of SEATO, it is certainly aligned with the West, and the two countries (with the Philippines) are loosely allied in the so-called Association of South-east Asia (formerly 'Association of South-east Asian States'). The two governments are strongly anti-communist.

With Burma, Thailand's relations are not unfriendly, despite the perennial problem of the Shan States. But Burma, as we have seen, is not the most stable of countries, and Thailand's enormously long frontier with a country of so uncertain a future is clearly a source of worry. Even more so, of course, is the long frontier with Laos, which stands in much greater danger of falling under communist control than Burma. There is already some guerrilla insurgency there.

It is perhaps scarcely surprising, then, that Thailand has aligned herself firmly with the West in SEATO, and has insisted that her integrity be guaranteed by the United States; during the Laotian crisis of 1962, American troops were sent into Thailand as an earnest of support. Meanwhile, Thailand benefits greatly from being the pivot of the Western alliance in South-east Asia. SEATO's headquarters are in Bangkok, and Thailand receives a great deal of American military aid. Indeed, it might be said that SEATO exists— as things have turned out—almost entirely to guarantee Thailand. And so long as the balance of advantage is clearly in favour of remaining aligned, Thailand will stay aligned.

It may well be that alignment, with American protection, is the only means by which Thailand's future independence can be guaranteed; at any rate, this is almost certainly what the Thais now believe. But it is possible to imagine circumstances in which non-alignment might appear to offer more advantages than alignment; and in that case the history of the Thais does not suggest that they will hesitate over-long before making the change.

6

Malaysia, Singapore and the Philippines

MALAYSIA AND SINGAPORE

THE Federation of Malaysia is a Commonwealth country consisting of three constituent parts: Malaya, which became independent in 1957 as a federation of eleven states in the Malayan peninsula formerly ruled or protected by Britain; and the former colonies of Sarawak and North Borneo (the latter being now called Sabah), which lie on the northern coast of the island of Borneo and have a land frontier nearly a thousand miles long with Kalimantan (Indonesian Borneo). From its inception in 1963 until August, 1965, Malaysia also included Singapore, the great island port at the southern tip of the peninsula.

Within the borders of Sarawak lies the tiny divided enclave state of Brunei, a British-protected sultanate which has not yet joined the Federation of Malaysia. Also in the area covered by this chapter is the Republic of the Philippines, a large archipelago lying to the north-east of Borneo. This became independent in 1946, after having been a colony first of Spain and then of the United States of America.

All these countries are, by Asian standards, prosperous. Whereas the *per capita* annual income of Indonesia was estimated in 1961 at only £11, that of Malaya was £97,* Sarawak's was £90, North Borneo's £75, and that of the Philippines £70.

This area, together with the Indonesian archipelago, is the homeland of the Malaysian peoples, with a large admixture of Chinese and Indian immigrants. Apart from the Dyaks

* The figure for Singapore was £150.

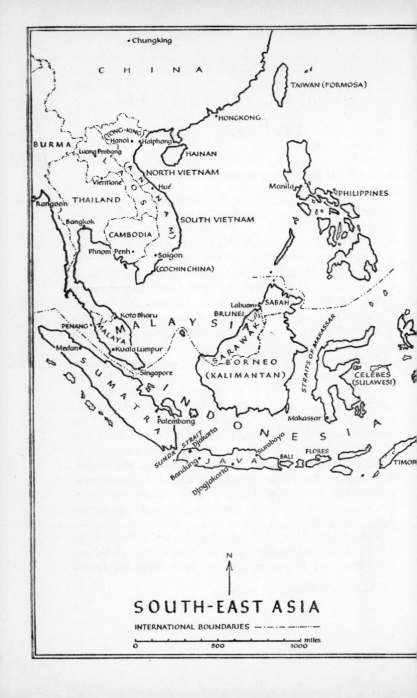

SOUTH-EAST ASIA

INTERNATIONAL BOUNDARIES ---·---·---·

miles
0   500   1000

of Borneo and some other inland races, the Malaysian peoples are for the most part coast-dwellers. The Malayan peninsula itself appears to have been inhabited for at least 5,000 years, yet something like four-fifths of the original Federation of Malaya is still covered by dense tropical jungle, the only generally cleared areas being in the north, the western states and some river valleys.

The eleven states of Malaya, which is slightly larger than England, have a total population of nearly 7½ million, of whom around half are Malays and more than a third Chinese. Singapore contains about 1¾ million people, of whom more than 1¼ million are Chinese by race. Sabah and Sarawak have populations of around half a million and three-quarters of a million respectively. Here the Malaysian races (though not the peninsula Malays) are in a clear majority, the Chinese representing about 30 per cent of the total. It was this which made the leaders of the peninsula Malays so anxious to secure the adherence of Sabah and Sarawak to the Federation of Malaysia, since the preponderance of Malaysians there helped to offset the big Chinese majority in Singapore and balance the racial structure of the new Federation.

The two parts of Brunei together contain some 100,000 people. The Republic of the Philippines has a population of over 28 million.

*   *   *

When the British and Dutch East India Companies supplanted the Portuguese as the dominant European traders in the East Indies soon after the beginning of the seventeenth century, it remained an open question for 200 years which of them would prevail. At first the Dutch established themselves in Java, Sumatra and other islands of the Indonesian archipelago, and ousted the British. British trade with southeast Asia continued, however, and in 1786 the need for a permanent trading centre and for a naval repair base led to the development of Penang, a small island just off the western coast of the Malayan peninsula. Soon afterwards, a tract of land facing Penang on the mainland (and later named Province Wellesley) was purchased, also from the Sultan of Kedah.

By the end of the century Britain was temporarily supreme. The French had overrun the Netherlands, whereupon the British occupied Dutch possessions in the East Indies, with the intention of handing them back to an independent Holland after the war. This temporary check to Dutch expansion lost them Malaya.

If Stamford Raffles, the great servant of the East India Company who became Lieutenant-Governor of Java in 1811, had had his way, the Dutch would have lost the East Indies as well. He envisaged a 'Greater Malaysia' in which British trading interests would be supreme. But neither the British Government nor the Company were in the mood for expansion south of the equator, and Raffles' suggestions were ill received—with one important exception. This was his determination that the Dutch must not be allowed to control both the vital approaches from the Indian Ocean to the China Seas. When Britain finally handed back the Dutch possessions in the East Indies in 1816, Holland controlled one of them, the Sunda Straits between Java and Sumatra. Raffles determined that Britain must secure control of the Straits of Malacca, between Sumatra and the Malay Peninsula.

On February 6, 1819, Raffles concluded a treaty with the Sultan of Johore, providing for the cession of the island of Singapore, then inhabited by some 500 seafaring Malays and a number of Chinese plantation workers. In little over a year the population of the new settlement had grown to nearly 5,000; trade was expanding rapidly, and the strategic importance of Singapore was obvious. Dutch protests made no impression on the British Government, and in 1824 the two countries reached a permanent understanding. The Dutch withdrew from the mainland of Asia, abandoning Malacca to the British, while the British recognised the East Indian islands as a Dutch sphere of interest.

In 1826 Penang, Singapore and Malacca were combined

to form the Straits Settlements, with Singapore as their capital. The dependency was governed from India until 1867. No attempt was made to acquire, or interfere in, the other states of the Malay peninsula until events forced the hands of the British many years later.

A number of factors combined to make it impossible to maintain the *status quo*. An expansionist Siam tried to establish suzerainty over the northern states of Malaya, and actually conquered Kedah as early as 1821. The seafaring Malays took to piracy on a large enough scale to alarm both British traders and the Chinese merchants who were developing Singapore and the other ports. The independent states of Malaya began to degenerate into anarchy, with civil war and dynastic murder becoming almost commonplace. Finally, the enormous development of tin-mining, and later of the rubber plantations, produced an economic revolution combined with a huge influx of Chinese and Indian immigrants which gave rise to problems with which the Malayan feudal system could no longer cope.

After 1873 British intervention was felt to be essential, not only for reasons of trade and economic development but —even more important—because it was feared that the decay of the Malayan states would allow another European power to gain a foothold on the peninsula. The Straits Settlements had become a Crown Colony in 1867. Gradually the independent states were brought under British protection and British 'Residents' appointed to them. In 1896 Perak, Selangor, Pahang and Negri Sembilan were brought together in the Federated Malay States; each retained its own British Resident, but a Resident-General was appointed at Kuala Lumpur, responsible to the Governor of the Straits Settlements. Johore became a protected state in 1885, and in 1909 Siam renounced her suzerainty over Kedah, Kelantan, Perlis and Trengganu, these states coming under British protection with a resident 'Adviser'.

*   *   *

Meanwhile a breach had been made in the agreement whereby the Dutch were to keep the East Indies islands as their unchallenged sphere of interest. They had not extended their control over the whole island of Borneo, and the northern coastal area remained independent under the Sultans of Brunei and Sulu. This area provided bases for many of the pirates who menaced the growing trade of the Straits.

The first British interest in Borneo was acquired by individual private enterprise. In 1838 James Brooke, a wealthy and able young adventurer who had served the East India Company and been greatly influenced by the ideas of Stamford Raffles, sailed in his own yacht for Brunei. There he helped the Sultan to put down a rebellion in Sarawak, of which he was made Governor in 1841. His measures against piracy led to trouble with the Sultan, and in 1846 Brooke (with the aid of the British navy) captured Brunei and imposed conditions which began the progressive destruction of the former greatness of the Sultanate. Brooke became sovereign Rajah of Sarawak; Brunei entered into a commercial treaty with Britain, and the offshore island of Labuan became a British dependency to be developed as a coaling station.

The former colony of British North Borneo owed its origin, strangely enough, to an American initiative in the middle of the nineteenth century, a large tract of Brunei and of the Sultan of Sulu's North Borneo possessions having been ceded to a company which finally came under British control. This company secured a Royal Charter in 1881 and, as the British North Borneo Company, ruled North Borneo from 1881 until the Japanese conquest in 1941 and Labuan from 1889 to 1906.

There was from the first territorial and commercial rivalry between the Chartered Company and the Brooke Rajahs of Sarawak, and the contracting Sultanate of Brunei was progressively squeezed between them. In 1888, at the request of the Company and against the will of both Brooke and the

Sultan of Brunei, a British protectorate was imposed on Brunei, North Borneo and Sarawak.

* * *

The administration of Malaya between the wars was complicated by its division into three sections—the Straits Settlements, Federated Malay States and unfederated states. A proposal in 1931—eminently sensible, if a little before its time—to unite them in a loose Pan-Malayan Union provoked uproar, and was rejected on the grounds that the so-called authority of the Malay Rulers must be preserved and that the Malays would be swamped by the Chinese and Indians. The British, uneasily aware that the Malays were the true native inhabitants of the peninsula and that British immigration policy had greatly worsened their position, took pains to safeguard what was left of Malay rights. Some Malays were educated for the Civil Service, and the rest were encouraged to continue their traditional way of life as subsistence peasant farmers and small planters of cash crops. Chinese and Indians worked the plantations and mined the tin, and also secured a stranglehold on commerce and moneylending.

Although this was storing up trouble for the future, it provoked no particular nationalist ferment or communal troubles. By Asian standards, apart from the rubber crisis in the slump of the early 1930s, Malaya was prosperous. A shadow of future trouble was seen when Chinese communists took over a strike of Chinese workers on the Selangor rubber estates a few years before the war and sought to foment both inter-racial strife and anti-colonialist agitation, but on the whole life proceeded peacefully until the Japanese conquest.

The fall of French Indo-China and a long train of miscalculations led to the rapid over-running of the peninsula by the Japanese in 1941–42 and the fall of Singapore. It was a crushing blow and quite unexpected. The Japanese brought Malaya to the verge of ruin, exploiting the people mercilessly and restoring the four northern states to Siam. (They were restored back to Malaya at the end of the war.) In Malaya, at least, the return of the British was greeted with genuine enthusiasm.

As in other countries, however, the years of occupation greatly strengthened the position of the communists. The Chinese communists in Malaya provided almost the only effective resistance, and they formed a focus of anti-colonial feeling which was much easier to foment when the Japanese were the colonialists. One unhappy result was the stirring up of a purely Chinese nationalism in Malaya, and the behaviour of some of the Chinese guerrillas greatly antagonised the Malays.

In the interval between Japanese withdrawal and the arrival of British troops, the communist guerrillas strengthened their position still further. Although they were politely disarmed and disbanded, caches of Japanese and British arms were carefully put down for future use. One incident at this time calls for special mention. A Chinese guerrilla leader named Chin Peng was profusely thanked and awarded the O.B.E. Ten years later, as leader of the communist insurgents in Malaya, he had a price of £20,000 on his head—and he is still in hiding on the Thai frontier awaiting another chance!

A brisk onslaught was made on the task of restoring the country from a state of economic chaos to a condition of prosperity with the rubber estates and tin mines functioning once more. By 1947 recovery was almost complete, despite a communist attempt to create strike chaos in Singapore; but in June, 1948, a state of emergency had to be declared owing to the communist guerrilla insurgency, and this slowed up both economic growth and progress towards self-government.

The situation did not begin to improve until the end of 1951, on the eve of General Templer's appointment as High Commissioner. From then on, progress was slow but sure, although the emergency did not end until 1960.

Meanwhile, the decision in 1946 to create a Union of the

whole peninsula except Singapore had again alarmed the Malays, and the United Malays National Organisation (UMNO) was formed under the leadership of Dato Onn (succeeded in 1951 by Tunku Abdul Rahman). Early in 1949 the Malayan Chinese Association (MCA) was formed under Dato Tan Cheng-lock, a wealthy Chinese rubber magnate. Although MCA was largely a party of the better-off commercial Chinese, with no broad popular base, it performed a valuable service in genuinely seeking to heal the widening breach between Malays and Chinese.

When Malaya became a Federation in 1948, the citizenship laws gave Malays a great advantage, since all Malaysians (even Indonesian immigrants) automatically secured citizenship, while the Chinese and Indians had to have family roots in Malaya. This gave the Malays a political advantage, and MCA's strategy was to concede this as a price for securing maintenance of Chinese economic dominance. Although scarcely a sound basis for the future, this enabled UMNO and MCA to come together in 1953 in the Alliance, which greatly strengthened Tunku Abdul Rahman's hands in negotiating with the British for independence.

This, after much British havering about terms, was secured in September, 1957, when the Federation of Malaya joined the Commonwealth as a self-governing state. The Tunku,* whose UMNO-MCA Alliance had won all but one of the 52 elective seats in the old Federal Assembly in 1955, became Prime Minister. The constituent states retained some measure of internal autonomy, and the Federation has a Supreme Head of State (in fact a King) elected for a five-year term by the hereditary rulers of the states from among their numbers.

Britain continued aid for external defence and internal security, and a Commonwealth Strategic Reserve including United Kingdom, Australian and New Zealand Army and Air Force units is stationed in Malaya.

* It is technically incorrect to call Tunku Abdul Rahman '*the Tunku*', but it has become common usage.

The new Government, while pressing ahead with the creation of a completely native administration—into which, even before Alliance rule, non-Malays were being admitted—deliberately retained the services of many senior British civil servants and experts. The policy was one of sure, rather than revolutionary progress, and it has paid dividends.

In 1959, the Alliance parties, which by now included also the Malayan Indian Congress, won 74 of the 104 new parliamentary seats. There had been some trouble over the allotment of seats to the MCA, who demanded 35 candidates to UMNO's 67 or so; in the end, somewhat unwillingly, it accepted 31 to UMNO's 69 and the MIC's 4. It was estimated that the number of Chinese electors had increased from 155,000 in 1955 to around 750,000, and the proportion of non-Malay electors was very much larger (it is still growing).

Despite the large amounts of foreign capital invested in Malaya, and the Government's concentration of development aid on improving the position of country Malays, the very rapid growth in Malaya's prosperity meant a further growth in the wealth and economic influence of the middle-class Chinese, at a time when their political influence was also growing with the size of their electoral role. Inter-racial suspicions and tensions began to increase.

It was these that had prevented the incorporation into the Federation of the Crown Colony of Singapore, whose 1¼ million Chinese would, the Malays feared, swamp them. But the separation of Singapore, with its British base and huge Asian entrepôt trade, was obviously absurd. Tunku Abdul Rahman's thoughts began to turn towards the idea of a federation which would include not only Singapore but the colonies of north Borneo as well, to balance the racial structure.

*   *   *

Singapore had become a separate British colony in 1946, with a partly elective Legislative Council; in the 1948 and

1951 elections, however, the Chinese virtually boycotted the poll. In 1955 the colony obtained a measure of self-government, the Governor having substantial reserve powers for use in any emergency threatening the important British base.

The first Chief Minister was David Marshall, an eloquent lawyer of Anglo-Indian stock, leading the Labour Front. Plagued by labour troubles at home and unable to reach agreement with the British on terms for complete self-government, Mr Marshall resigned in 1956. His successor was Lim Yew-hock, a Malayan Chinese with a wider appeal to the people of Singapore. He was able to deal more effectively with communist-inspired labour troubles, and also finally negotiated terms for independence. A compromise was reached for securing the British base, through the establishment of an Internal Security Council of three Singapore Ministers, three British representatives and a representative of the Federation of Malaya with a casting vote.

The British, alarmed by the activities of the communists and of the far-left People's Action Party (PAP), insisted that at the first elections no political leader under detention at the time of the agreement should stand as a candidate.

However, when elections took place in May, 1959, on a basis of universal suffrage, the PAP won 43 out of 51 seats. The first Prime Minister of nearly-independent Singapore was the PAP leader Lee Kuan-yew, a tough, able, shrewd and patriotic politician. He came of the third generation of a prosperous Straits Chinese merchant family, and took a law degree at Cambridge.

Mr Lee met with his full share of troubles. He was determined to end inter-racial strife and placate the Malays, but had to do it without forfeiting his majority Chinese support. He was determined to thwart the growing ambitions and trade-union support of the communists, and to out-manœuvre them he had to appear pretty far out on the left himself, which tended to alarm the wealthier Chinese as well as the British and Malayan Governments.

The real trouble soon made itself plain. Crypto-communists had infiltrated his own PAP, and he was continually at odds with these extremists. Their activities were particularly embarrassing to Lee Kuan-yew since he had already set his heart on federation with Malaya and was anxious not to alarm the right-wing parties of the peninsula.

In 1961 he suffered two serious setbacks. A former PAP Minister, Ong Eng-guan, who had previously been a militantly anti-British mayor of Singapore, came out in violent opposition to the Prime Minister and won a crushing victory in a by-election against a PAP candidate. Two months later the individualist David Marshall made a flamboyant reappearance on the scene and won another by-election.

Some of Mr Lee's extreme left-wingers deserted him, and the rest he expelled from the PAP. They formed the *Barisan Sosialis* (Socialist Front), with 14 M.P.s. Mr Lee's majority was crumbling.

Paradoxically, this made Tunku Abdul Rahman more, rather than less, inclined to the Malayan-Singapore merger which Mr Lee now urgently needed. The Tunku took the view that Malaya's interests would be better served by absorbing Singapore, despite the difficulties of racial balance and the fears of the peninsula Malays, than by letting Singapore slide into communism. The Tunku and Mr Lee got together and got on extremely well. Terms were agreed between them, and British approval secured. In October, 1961, the Malayan Parliament agreed to the scheme in principle. The Singapore Assembly debated the proposed terms on November 20; the *Barisan Sosialis* and other opposition members, after violent attacking speeches (Dr Liew Siew-choh's lasted for $7\frac{1}{2}$ hours), balked at the possible unpopularity to be incurred by voting against it and walked out. The motion was carried, with Alliance support, by 33 votes to nil.

Lee Kuan-yew now had to survive until federation became a reality, which was not until September, 1963. It was touch-and-go, but he made it—largely by sailing into the *Barisan Sosialis* and communists and putting most of them under arrest. No doubt he had learned the technique from the Tunku.

*　*　*

Meanwhile the centre of interest in the struggle to achieve the federation of 'Greater Malaysia' had shifted to the north of the island of Borneo. It was proposed that the protected Sultanate of Brunei, together with Sarawak and British North Borneo (to be known as Sabah), should join the federation to balance the Chinese of Singapore with the more-or-less Malaysian majority in their territories. Not all the Dyaks, Dusuns and other Borneo races were enthusiastic about union with the peninsula Malays and there was opposition in Sarawak.

The decision in respect of Sabah and Sarawak lay with the British Government. After the war, faced with the repair of the devastation left by the Japanese, the United Kingdom had resumed British North Borneo from the Chartered Company, and persuaded Rajah Brooke to cede Sarawak; both were now Crown Colonies, taking the first leisurely colonial steps towards self-government. The tiny divided enclave of Brunei was still ruled by the Sultan, who profited richly from oil royalties, and up to 1959 had a British Resident. In 1959 a new constitution promised partially elective government, and in August, 1962, all the elective seats were won by the Partai Ra'ayat Brunei, led by Sheikh Azahari, an Indonesian-trained megalomaniac.

The British Government approved the federation, but decided to proceed with caution to avert Asian accusations of 'neo-colonialism'. A claim to Sabah by the Philippines, as the 'successor state' to the Sultan of Sulu, was not taken very seriously, but a weather eye was kept on the reactions of Indonesia. President Sukarno was known to believe that if anyone were to unite 'Greater Malaysia' it ought to be himself; but he was at the time engaged in blackmailing the Dutch to disgorge western New Guinea, and on November 20, 1961, his Foreign Minister, Dr Subandrio, explicitly told the UN General Assembly that Indonesia had no claims on the North Borneo territories and wished the new federation success.

Nevertheless, the British and Malayan Governments took the precaution of appointing a joint commission under the chairmanship of Lord Cobbold, which painstakingly canvassed opinion in the backwoods of Sabah and Sarawak and pronounced that a majority of the people were in favour of the merger. This view was supported by political results in the territories. Later in 1962, Lee Kuan-yew held a (fairly free) referendum in Singapore, which decisively approved the terms.

But by now Sukarno had won his battle for Dutch New Guinea and was looking for another great external cause to keep his communists happy and distract Indonesian attention from the appalling economic chaos at home. Just as if Dr Subandrio had never uttered at the UN in 1961, Sukarno opened up his campaign of "confrontation" with Malaysia. His intention was—and is—specifically to gain control of the northern territories beyond the Indonesian frontier in Borneo, and ultimately to become the leader of the Pan-Malaysia that his megalomaniac and unpractical mind dreams of.

He did not move directly at first, having a tool at hand. In December, 1962, Sheikh Azahari of Brunei launched an armed revolt—with Indonesian-trained forces—which spread into parts of Sarawak and Sabah. Indeed, he proclaimed his intention to 'liberate' these territories, and announced that he was Prime Minister of the 'Revolutionary State of North Kalimantan' (Kalimantan being the Indonesian name for Borneo). He did not stay Prime Minister for long; and, although he wisely directed his revolt from Manila in the Philippines, it was to Djakarta in Indonesia that he fled when it was crushed in a week by British and Malayan forces. He is still there—head of a 'revolutionary government in exile'. He had achieved one thing. The Sultan of Brunei, already unwilling to surrender his sovereignty and claiming that the oil royalty terms were unsatisfactory, decided not to join the federation.

Sukarno now took up the (verbal) cudgels himself. The Malaysia which Dr Subandrio had wished so well in 1961 was now, early in 1963, a neo-colonialist plot to preserve the imperialists' economic interests and military bases. Egged on by the communists, he became more and more violent. By April, he was to all intents and purposes at war.

The original nucleus of the 'confrontation' forces was Azahari's Tentara Nasional Kalimantan Utara (TNKU), or National Army of North Kalimantan, swollen by communists and other dissidents from Brunei, Sabah and Sarawak. But these 'volunteers', trained in jungle warfare and sea-borne infiltration by the Indonesian Army, proved inadequate in numbers and fighting spirit when Sukarno wanted the pace hotted up. In April, 1963, raids into Sarawak were started, spreading to Sabah in October. By the end of the year Indonesian regular army personnel were being used in increasing numbers.

The operations were distinguished by the pathetically ramshackle incompetence which is a feature of Sukarno's Indonesia. Inadequately trained, badly briefed, and assured that the imperialists' exploited subjects would welcome them with open arms, the wretched volunteers were landed on, or pushed into, hostile territory (often in the wrong places) only to be rapidly mopped up by British and Malayan security forces or slaughtered by infuriated Dyaks.

Nevertheless, the nuisance value of the raids was—and remains—enormous. It is by now a commonplace fact of South-east Asian life that one subversive guerrilla fighter needs ten to twelve government soldiers to contain him; and when Indonesia can switch its raiding points along a 1,000-mile land frontier in Borneo (and now along the coasts of Singapore and the Peninsula), very large security forces are required to counter them. It is a heavy strain on both the United Kingdom and Malaysia.

Despite Sukarno's bluster and force, the Federation of

Malaysia, consisting of Malaya, Singapore, Sarawak and Sabah, came into being in September, 1963. Tunku Abdul Rahman leaned over backwards—with an eye on neutralist Asian opinion—to meet all Sukarno's points. Having from the first refused to align Malaya in SEATO, he announced that Singapore could not be used by the British for SEATO purposes once it joined Malaysia. He met Sukarno in Manila in July, 1963, when President Macapagal of the Philippines mediated.

The Tunku, keeping his temper well under control, even agreed to postpone the proclamation of Malaysia until a UN mission had made sure that the people of Sabah and Sarawak wanted it. He also agreed to join a loose kind of confederation with Indonesia and the Philippines, to be known as Maphilindo. This never came to anything, because the UN mission duly found that the people of Sabah and Sarawak *did* want to join Malaysia, which infuriated Sukarno.

In January, 1964, Mr Robert Kennedy visited Djakarta and Kuala Lumpur as an American Government mediator. Sukarno was reported to have been pretty offensive to him, but promised to call a cease-fire for negotiations. He broke the promise; and in June, at more 'summit' talks in Tokyo, he finally refused to withdraw his Borneo guerrillas. In January, 1965, Indonesia left the UN as an anti-Malaysia protest.

So it goes on. And it has spread from Borneo to Singapore and the peninsula. From bomb outrages and other acts of sabotage, Indonesia has proceeded to direct raids on Malayan and Singapore territory. There is also a steady campaign of subversion and incitement to inter-racial strife in Malaysia. The communists are active in this, and reap most of the benefits. After federation, Indonesia also closed off Indonesian entrepôt trade through Singapore.

In the end Sukarno scored another indirect success, to set beside the withdrawal of Brunei from the federation plan. It was not actually his own actions which precipitated the break-up between Malaya and Singapore in August, 1965, but 'confrontation' certainly helped to create the atmosphere in which the break occurred.

In fact, the right-wing Malay nationalists virtually drove Singapore out of Malaysia. They made of Malaysia yet another episode in the tragic catalogue of Commonwealth federations that failed. In logic, Malaya and Singapore belong together. There was every reason—economic, geographical and strategic—why Malaysia should have succeeded. It foundered—for the time being, at least—on inter-racial fears and suspicions.

The nationalist peninsula Malay politicians had always feared the arrival of Singapore's Chinese in a situation in which Malayan political influence on the mainland was already threatened with decline. In particular, they feared Lee Kuan-yew. They had 'done a deal' with the prosperous Malayan Chinese through the MCA, which remained a loyal member of the Alliance. But the MCA had no more broad popular support among the coolie Chinese than before. What if the astute and attractive Mr Lee, with a foot in the peninsula after federation, should make himself the popular leader of the Chinese masses in Malaya? Then the Chinese might well become politically dominant. That the MCA also feared Mr Lee was shown by the attacks on him in 1965 by their normally moderate leader, Finance Minister Tan Siew Sin.

So, against the will of Tunku Abdul Rahman—who appeared in mid-1965 to be for the first time losing control of his right-wing supporters—and to the despair of the unhappy Mr Lee, who saw all his massive achievements brought to nothing and a hideously complex task facing him, Singapore was forced out of Malaysia and became once more an independent state within the Commonwealth.

The questions raised were endless. Would Indonesia call off 'confrontation'? (Answer: almost certainly, no.) Would Indonesian trade return to Singapore? What was to happen to the British base, which is an economic necessity to Singapore? (Mr Lee got in early with a caveat against its use for

SEATO purposes.) Would the British feel inclined to keep the base going? What would happen to Sabah and Sarawak? Could Singapore remain viable on its own? Would the logic of federation reassert itself and Malaysia in the end be revived? If so, when?

At the time of writing none of these questions can be answered with confidence. What can be said is that, despite the prosperity of Malaya, future prospects are much less happy than they once looked. At the time of independence it was the most stable, as well as the most prosperous country in South-east Asia. The shadows over its future have been cast by racialism and by the purely and utterly destructive activities of President Sukarno.

THE PHILIPPINES

The Philippine archipelago consists of some 7,000 islands, most of them tiny and only a dozen important, stretching for 1,100 miles off the coasts of Asia. Their strategic importance can be gauged from the fact that the islands stretch from a point only 65 miles from Formosa to within 45 miles of Indonesia. The growing population is now more than 28 million.

It has been estimated that in this population there are 43 identifiable ethnic groups, with 87 languages. Rather more than 90 per cent of the population is at least nominally Christian, and 80 per cent are Roman Catholic. Some still speak Spanish, although probably a quarter or more of the people speak English. The overseas Chinese minority is more intermarried and assimilated than in most Asian countries.

Basically, though much crossed and diluted, the majority of the population are more or less Malaysian. When Magellan discovered the Philippines in 1521 and Spain conquered them in 1565, they were inhabited by the descendants of sea-faring Malays who had ousted the aboriginal Negritos and Indonesians. For more than 300 years the Spaniards ruled the islands, leaving an indelible mark upon them. But Filipino nationalism was growing at the end of the nineteenth century, and a revolutionary situation existed when the colonialist Americans put a stop to it by annexing the Philippines at the end of the Spanish-American War in 1899.

The motive for annexation, wrapped up in the usual high-minded talk about the Filipinos being unfit for self-government and needing to be taken care of, was purely strategic. Britain and Japan were happy to agree to it, because it kept the Germans out. But the Filipino nationalists, having been on the point of winning independence for themselves, were extremely cross. Despite a benevolent paternalistic rule and much social improvement, the nationalists battled on for self-government, led by Manuel Quezon. But history followed the usual colonialist pattern, with the Filipinos never being judged quite 'ready for independence', while United States enterprises secured a profitable economic stranglehold on the country.

Finally, in 1934, the Roosevelt Government granted a measure of internal self-government for a period of ten years, after which the Philippines were to become independent. Quezon became the first Filipino President, ruling like a pocket dictator under the American aegis. By 1941 there was a desperate economic crisis. But by the end of 1941 the Japanese had arrived.

The fall of Manila was a shock to the Filipinos as traumatic as the fall of Singapore to others. The invincible Western power had been beaten by an Asian conqueror. President Quezon, ordered to take his Government—against his will—to the United States, might guess that independence was assured after the war. The Philippines certainly fared no better at the hands of the Japanese than other Southeast Asian countries, but there seems to have been rather more than the normal number of collaborators. But there was also a resistance movement. Indeed, the communist-led Huks (Hukbalahaps, or People's Anti-Japanese Army) on Luzon went on resisting the Americans after the war.

For it seemed that the collaborators had won. After

American forces had regained the Philippines in a series of gallant and bloody actions, Quezon's deputy, Sergio Osmena, returned as President after Quezon's death. But independence was finally conceded in 1946, and the victors in the first general election were the Liberals, heavily backed in a not too cleanly democratic campaign by all the Manila collaborators. The new President Roxas was himself widely accused of collaboration.

The Huks had been technically disbanded by General MacArthur in 1945, but they had cached a fair supply of arms, and after the elections their leader, Luis Taruc, brought them into action again. It was soon a full-scale communist insurrection, and by 1948 the Huks controlled a substantial slice of Luzon. When President Roxas died in 1948 and the ensuing Quirino régime proved even more corrupt and incompetent, their support grew. It was not until 1954 that the Huk rebellion was finally broken, through the skill and energy of Defence Minister Ramon Magsaysay, who became President in 1953. This was the most hopeful event of recent Filipino history, but unfortunately Magsaysay—after having taken the Philippines into SEATO—was killed in an air crash in 1957.

Under his successor, President Garcia, corruption broke all records, and he was ousted at the 1961 elections by Diosdado Macapagal. Elected on an anti-corruption platform, he did not seem to reduce it markedly. Despite substantial U.S. aid (for which substantial trading advantages have been secured), the peasants remain poor and there is fairly heavy unemployment. The Philippines have never been a very efficient country. Anti-Americanism seems to be on the increase among the middle classes.

It was to be expected that the communists would take advantage of such a situation, and they have—directed both from China and from Indonesia. In 1965 there were reports that the Huks were on the move again in Luzon. The new President Ferdinand Marcos, who beat Macapagal in the 1965 elections, inherited a discouraging situation.

7
Indonesia

THERE is little doubt that Indonesia is the 'problem country' of South-east Asia. Its future is one large question-mark. Indo-China has no doubt been more in the news in the years since 1950, because of its obvious strategic importance and because Laos and North Vietnam lie on the land frontiers of communist China. But Indonesia has a population well over five times as large as those of these two countries put together, besides being potentially one of the richest countries in Asia.

Its strategic importance is also considerable, since it forms a 'barrier' between the Indian Ocean and the Pacific and between Asia and Australia. At one end the Indonesian archipelago lies within less than 50 miles of Singapore and Malaya, at the other it is barely 250 miles from Australia.

The Republic of Indonesia embraces the whole of the former Netherlands Indies with the exception of West New Guinea. The archipelago stretches no less than 3,300 miles from east to west and 1,300 miles from north to south. Its land area is 733,000 square miles, but it sprawls over a total area of the earth's surface nearly four times as large.

Some 3,000 of its islands are inhabited, although by far the biggest land areas are the islands of Java, Sumatra and Celebes (Sulawesi), together with the southern part of the island of Borneo (Kalimantan), where Indonesia has land frontiers with the former British colonies of Sarawak and North Borneo (now part of Malaysia). Smaller but important islands are Bangka and Billiton, which produce tin; Timor, part of which is still a Portuguese colony; and Bali, Madura, and the Moluccas (once known as the Spice Islands). The population is around 104 million, of which no less than two-thirds is concentrated in the single island of Java, and it appears to be increasing at the rate of about 1½ million a year

So great are Indonesia's natural resources that it seems almost unbelievable that the Government should have managed to keep the country in a state of poverty and economic confusion for so long. Apart from the traditional exports of pepper, nutmeg, cinnamon and other spices, Indonesia was before the war by far the world's greatest exporter of kapok and cinchona (quinine) bark, and a substantial exporter of copra, palm oil, fibres, timber, rubber, tea, coffee and sugar; it is potentially capable of meeting the whole demand for rice from its growing population. It was also, before the war, exporting large quantities of tin and petroleum, and was a substantial producer of bauxite, coal, nickel, manganese, sulphur, gold and silver. Even in times when world prices of raw materials (especially agricultural products) are low, Indonesia is potentially a very wealthy country.

* * *

The history of Indonesia is long and fascinating. Java, indeed, seems to have been one of the birthplaces of the human species, for it was there that the bones were discovered of *Pithecanthropus erectus*, an evolving hominid of the Lower Quaternary period. In later ages the archipelago underwent the usual 'southward drive' of various races from the north, each fresh wave tending to drive its predecessors further eastwards along the chain of islands, until perhaps some of the earlier races reached Australia. The Malaysians, not until quite recently a very numerous race, arrived about 4,000 years ago. The first major cultural influence was Indo-Aryan, bringing Brahman Hinduism and Sanskrit. Then, again from India, came Buddhism, which has left on the plain of central Java what was perhaps the most splendid architectural achievement in all its history—the breath-taking temple of Borobudur. Finally, again from India, came Islam in the fourteenth century of our era. This is the faith of Indonesia today.

The Indian cultures inspired the rise of local empires.

Srivijaya spread its influence from Sumatra, giving way in the fourteenth century to the already flourishing Javanese empire of Madjapahit. The Indo-Javanese civilisation was remarkable for its culture, which has left an abiding legacy to Indonesia (although perhaps the most persistent Indian strain has been that which inspired the idiosyncratic Hindu culture of Bali).

Indonesia was left more or less untouched by the Mongols and Chinese, and the next historical influence upon it was that of Europe, which began with the arrival of the Portuguese in Malacca in 1511. After Philip II of Spain conquered Portugal, the way became open for the newly independent Dutch to take over Portuguese possessions in the east. Despite the rivalry of the English, which was finally discouraged by the drastic method of arresting the staff of the East India Company on the island of Amboina in 1623 and putting them to death after torture, the Dutch secured that firm hold on the Indonesian archipelago that was to last until the middle of the twentieth century.

The Dutch have always been a single-minded people. They came to the Indies to trade, and for two and a half centuries they exploited them with quiet thoroughness, without totally conquering and pacifying the archipelago and certainly without much thought of improving the conditions of its inhabitants.

Towards the end of the nineteenth century public opinion in Holland became ashamedly aware of the nature of the exploitation of Java which had so markedly enriched the Dutch treasury. Economic development was gradually handed over to private enterprise, but the government at last began to bring the outer areas under control and to care for the interests of the peoples of Indonesia. Being Dutch, they were thorough, but they were also rather late. Only in the last ten years before the Japanese invasion did the government make a real effort to develop the Indonesian economy in the interests of the Indonesians and to encourage their co-operation in the task.

When the Japanese conquered Indonesia, they found a nationalist movement already in being and used it to destroy the influence of the Dutch. The intellectual leaders of this movement had for the most part been interned by the Dutch authorities at various times between 1927 and 1935. They included the moderate and scholarly Mohammed Hatta, the right-wing socialist Sutan Sjahrir, and an emotional young demagogue named Sukarno,* of mixed Javanese and Balinese parentage, who had in 1927 (at the age of 26) founded the *Partai Nasional Indonesia* (PNI) in Bandung.

These leaders resorted to different methods after the Japanese conquest: Sukarno's official apologists today assert that his collaboration with the Japanese was arranged by agreement with the other nationalists, and there may well have been some consultation. At all events, Sukarno and Hatta collaborated, becoming in 1943 virtually Japanese puppets. Sjahrir, on the other hand, 'went underground' to organise resistance, assisted by the left-wing socialist Amir Sjahrifuddin, and in the later stages of the war bitterly attacked Sukarno for the extent of his collaboration.

When the Japanese were on the verge of defeat in 1945, they set what has been described as a 'political time-bomb' in Indonesia by proclaiming the country's independence and turning over arms to the Javanese nationalists. Sukarno and Hatta promptly had themselves elected President and Vice-President respectively of a new republic of Indonesia. From this point onwards conditions began to become chaotic, a process which can scarcely be said to have ceased at the time of writing. British troops were given the task of occupying Indonesia, disarming the Japanese and re-patriating prisoners of war, but they had quite insufficient forces for so large a task and were forced to seek the co-operation of the Republican leaders. This annoyed the

* Sukarno, like many Indonesians, has only one name. Despite the efforts of incredulous Western journalists to provide him with a fore-name, he is not in fact either Abdul or Ahmed, but just plain Sukarno.

Dutch, who considered that collaborationist traitors had thus been given countenance. To add to the confusion, Sukarno and his colleagues claimed to represent the whole people of Indonesia, but were unable to make this large claim good. In the event, after some fighting and much argument, the Dutch recognised the authority of the Republic over Java, Sumatra and Madura (which contain about 80 per cent of the population), as part of a United States of Indonesia associated with Holland and under some measure of Dutch sovereignty.

The lack of sympathy between the Dutch and the Indonesian nationalists was almost total, and neither side seems to have made any great effort to make the agreement work. To be fair to the nationalists, neither President Sukarno nor his Prime Minister Sjahrir was in any position to control his extremist supporters. In addition, Sukarno and Sjahrir were at odds about the Republican form of government; Sukarno—perhaps naturally—favoured a strong Presidential executive such as the 1945 constitution had seemed to envisage, while Sjahrir manœuvred constitutional development along the lines of Western parliamentary democracy.

Political parties began to become effective. Sukarno's PNI was revived; Masjumi, a large Islamic party, gained much support among the peasants; the Socialists (PSI) attracted the intellectuals, but tended to splits between left and right; finally, the formerly outlawed communist PKI began to forge ahead in conditions almost ready-made for subversion.

Disagreements between Indonesians and Dutch over the territories outside the Republic grew more and more acrimonious. In July, 1947, soon after the crypto-communist Amir Sjahrifuddin had succeeded Sjahrir as Prime Minister, the Dutch made a more or less uncalled-for (and certainly unwise) attack on Republican territory. This 'police action', as the Dutch called it, produced a flurry of United Nations activity and protests from left-wing governments all over the world. Despite any amount of well-intentioned mediation, little progress was made after the cease-fire. A form of agreement was signed by Dutch and Republicans in January, 1948, but the immediate result was political chaos.

The PNI and Masjumi rejected the agreement. Sjahrifuddin's government fell, and he and his followers openly went over to the communists, who were much strengthened and encouraged; Sukarno seized the opportunity to get a firmer grip on the government of the Republic and set up Hatta as Prime Minister, who promptly accepted the Dutch agreement which had provoked the crisis. In September a communist rebellion at Madiun in Java, under a recently returned exile named Muso, who had assumed leadership of the PKI, was forcibly suppressed by the new Republican army. Muso was killed in action and Sjahrifuddin shot after capture. In December the Dutch launched a second 'police action', this time capturing the temporary Republican capital of Jogjakarta and arresting Sukarno, Hatta, Sjahrir and other leaders.

At this stage it is probable that the Dutch, if left to themselves, could have broken the Republic completely. With the dividing tactics of which they had already shown themselves masters, ruling the majority of the archipelago presented little difficulty, and their main forces could have been concentrated on Java with a fair prospect of success. How long they could have held the position is another matter; the forces of Indonesian nationalism in Java were pretty strong, and it is probable that they would have faced the prospect of intermittent guerrilla war on a scale that no small European country on the other side of the world could have afforded for very long. But in the event they were not left to themselves. To the great indignation of the Dutch they were assailed not only by all the newly independent countries of Asia but by their Western allies as well. Holland still feels hurt about this, and the subsequent story of West New Guinea has done nothing to heal the wound.

United Nations pressure forced the Dutch to evacuate Jogjakarta and release the Republican leaders at the end of June, 1949. There was now practically no hope of any friendly accommodation between the two sides. Despite Dutch attempts to carry off something like the original federal conception under the suzerainty of Holland, the independence of Indonesia was assured. In 1950 the pretence of federalism was dropped, and the Republic of Indonesia was proclaimed as a unitary state, Mohammad Natsir of Masjumi succeeding Hatta as its first Prime Minister. Finally the formal union with Holland was also dissolved.

All this was not achieved without some opposition, which included the dramatic attempt by Captain 'Turco' Westerling and other ex-members of the Netherlands East Indies Army to overthrow the Republican Government, and similar revolts in Makassar and the South Moluccas. There had also been another flurry of communist insurgency, under an unscrupulous agitator named Tan Malaka, who was shot.

Meanwhile, parliamentary government was undergoing the usual trials and strains of new Asian countries. One cabinet succeeded another, mostly coalitions between PNI and Masjumi; attempted reforms in 1952–53 were thwarted by Sukarno and by the Army. In October, 1952, a crowd of 5,000 demonstrators in Batavia—now renamed Djakarta and the capital of the Republic—demanded the dissolution of Parliament and a more efficient government. The Chief of Staff of the Army, a young colonel named Abdul Haris Nasution (of whom much more was to be heard in the fullness of time), was accused of instigating the demonstration and dismissed from his post.

The inefficiency and corruption of the Republican administration could fairly be laid at the door of the Dutch, who had made only the most belated attempts to educate and train

Indonesians for responsible positions. One of the results of this was that the achievement of power seemed to go to the heads of some of its possessors, producing irresponsibility and a certain political *folie de grandeur* which ran to sweeping concepts and large plans rather than to efficiency and detailed policies.

It cannot be said that President Sukarno has set the most helpful of examples in this respect. He has carried *charisma* to the point at which he sometimes seems to have lost touch completely with reality. The more chaotic economic conditions inside Indonesia have become, the larger has been the sweep of the plans and projects emanating from the President's impressive palaces in Djakarta and Bogor. When things became too difficult even to be palliated by progressive expropriations of foreign property, he has fallen back on three expedients: first, high-sounding constitutional changes which concentrate more power in his own hands, accompanied by passionate (almost paranoiac) speeches to mass rallies and promises of rapid solutions; second, attempts to regenerate the Spirit of the Revolution, generally by preaching a crusade against an outside enemy (e.g. the 'liberation' of West Irian, more recently the 'confrontation' with Malaysia, with Portuguese Timor no doubt next on the list); finally, when all else is exhausted, he has set off on a glamorous and much publicised 'goodwill tour' abroad.

Nevertheless, when all this (and much more) is said, the achievements of Sukarno have also to be weighed in the balance. Indonesia *has* secured her independence and, despite all the odds against it, she *has* remained united at least in form. When the fantastic sprawl of the archipelago and the diversity of its peoples and interests are considered, this is remarkable in all the circumstances. There are those who maintain that it has been achieved rather in spite of Sukarno than because of him, but this is surely going too far. He was certainly a great revolutionary leader, a little in the Castro style but with more to him than this suggests. He handled the campaign to win independence from the Dutch, and to unite the country in the first place, with very great skill. His contention, to which he held consistently from the beginning, that Western parliamentary democracy would not work in the early years of independence, proved to be correct. His political philosophy, a blend of moderate socialism and the ancient Malaysian ideal of *gotong rojong* (mutual help), was theoretically well suited to the country's needs.

Above all, he was able until 1965 to retain popular support and to balance powers and interests (such as the Army and the communists, for example) without allowing either to get out of hand. If only he had shown the least understanding of, or interest in, his country's economic problems he would have been a great leader, for the neutralist policy he pursued after 1952 enabled Indonesia to retain the goodwill of both East and West and to draw economic aid from both blocs. But this strange irresponsibility, which seeems to have been increasing in recent years, has been an almost fatal flaw in his achievements. Whether the country, which certainly needs leadership concentrated on its real problems, could in fact hang together without him is the great question-mark over its future.

Sukarno's major contribution to Indonesia's political development has been the concept of 'Guided Democracy', and it may be said that the country's politicians soon made it abundantly clear that they were incapable of making the unguided kind work. At the first general elections in September, 1955, no fewer than 28 political parties took part. At one time there were 40 parties all claiming national status. Four parties won most of the 257 seats in 1955: the PNI (57); Masjumi (57); Nahdatul Ulama ('Muslim Scholars', or NU, a party with marked anti-Western leanings) won 45 seats; and the communist PKI won 39. Sukarno attempted to negotiate the formation of a coalition of all four parties, but the others would not work with the PKI, which was consequently left out of the government. The resulting cabinet took the first major step against Dutch economic interests in May, 1956 (while Sukarno was absent on a goodwill tour abroad), as a reprisal for the Dutch refusal to surrender West New Guinea ('West Irian') to Indonesia.

In 1957 Indonesia began to show clear signs of falling apart. Especially in Sumatra and Sulawesi, there was much dissatisfaction and jealousy directed against the privileged position of Java. Several local military commanders took over the administration of their areas and began to withhold taxes and encourage a form of local 'free trade' which amounted to a large-scale smuggling operation. The Masjumi politicians resigned from the government in sympathy with the demands for local autonomy, and Sukarno took his first step towards 'Guided Democracy' by setting up what was described as an 'emergency extra-parliamentary cabinet of experts' under Djuanda Kartawidjaja.

A National Council was also set up, with Sukarno as chairman; the vice-chairman and secretary-general was a former Foreign Minister, Ruslan Abdulgani, who later achieved a dominant position among the politicians. Members of the communist PKI participated in the National Council, but not in the cabinet.

None of this did anything to reassure the Army dissidents. On November 30 the first attempt was made to assassinate Sukarno in Djakarta; on December 17 a national 'state of war' was proclaimed, and on January 6, 1958, the President set out on another goodwill tour abroad; during his absence, open rebellion broke out.

For the next $3\frac{1}{2}$ years there were always rebels fighting somewhere in Indonesia, and it is by no means certain that West Java is wholly pacified yet. Not all the risings were inspired by the same objectives, and they were far from being co-ordinated. There were military revolts under Lieutenant-Colonel Ahmad Hussein in Sumatra, where a so-called 'Revolutionary Government' (known as the PRRI) was proclaimed, and under Colonel Kawilarang in north and central Sulawesi. Fighting also broke out in the Moluccas.

Perhaps the most significant feature of what was on the whole a rather amateur revolutionary movement was the formal adherence to the rebels of Dr Sjafruddin Prawirane-gara, a former minister and at that time Governor of the Bank of Indonesia, and Dr Sumitro Djojohadikusumo, a former Finance Minister; at the same time Hatta and Sjahrir, Sukarno's respected associates of the independence movement, clearly indicated their lack of support for the President. Thus the government lost the support of virtually the only men who had ever shown any signs of being able to cope with the country's economic problems. It has not yet found a sub-stitute. Even moderate and patriotic nationalists like the Sultan of Jogjakarta have been alienated.

A later addition to the rebel ranks was the fanatical Darul Islam movement, dedicated to the creation of a theocratic Muslim state, which rose under Kahar Muzakkar in South Sulawesi and West Java. The Darul Islam fought on in Sula-wesi until October, 1961, when Kahar Muzakkar surrendered, and for much longer in the mountains of West Java.

Sumatra was brought under some sort of control as early as April, 1958, when the recently promoted General Nasution —restored to his former position of Army Chief of Staff— launched a competently executed combined operation against the rebels there, who did not seek to fight a pitched battle. However, guerrilla fighting continued in Sumatra until the middle of 1961. Perhaps the most determined military cam-paign was fought in North Sulawesi by Col. Kawilarang, formerly commander-in-chief in East Indonesia; he sur-rendered in March, 1961, but another leader, Col. Sumual, remained at large. So did Dr Sumitro, living as a refugee in Kuala Lumpur.

Early in January, 1959, doggedly pursuing his determina-tion to secure his 'Guided Democracy', Sukarno held a series of talks with PNI, NU and PKI leaders about what had already become dignified by the typically high-flown title of the 'President's Concept'. Agreement was reached on the essentials of the scheme, including the incorporation of the so-called 'functional groups' (representing, *inter alia*, peasants, trade unions, industry, the armed forces and teachers) in the proposed *Madjelis* or elected People's Assembly.

In April the President requested the Constituent Assembly to abolish the 1950 constitution and adopt the revolutionary constitution of 1945, which gave him the powers he sought and the framework for 'Guided Democracy'. The following day he left with a large entourage on the biggest goodwill tour of all, leaving the Assembly to wrestle with the problem of achieving the necessary two-thirds majority for a proposal which Masjumi and some of the smaller parties simply were not prepared to accept.

For two months it failed to reach agreement. On July 5 Sukarno, refreshed by his world tour, took the bull by the horns. Declaring that the Constituent Assembly had 'broken down', he dissolved it by decree 'in the name of the people of Indonesia' and announced that the 1945 constitution was in force. Four days later he became Prime Minister as well as President, Djuanda Kartawidjaja being renamed First Minister. He then proceeded to use his emergency powers to short-circuit elections during what was described as a 'transitional period' and appoint the members of all the executive and advisory bodies in the system of 'Guided Democracy'. All this was done with the agreement of the PNI, NU and PKI leaders, after which the President set off (on April 1, 1960) on a world goodwill tour.

On August 17, in the course of his annual Independence Day Speech, Sukarno made two more typical gestures. He announced that the Masjumi Party was banned and dissolved, together with the PSI (Socialists), thus ridding himself of the only two major parties which opposed him. The remainder were compulsorily amalgamated in a new 'National Front'. At the same time, in the course of a passionately demagogic harangue about the forthcoming 'liberation' of West Irian, he announced that diplomatic relations with Holland had been broken off. He had already used every other sanction against the Dutch without effect, repudiating debts, confiscating assets and nationalising plantations, industries and ships; in the long run, this did the Indonesian economy more harm than good, since the Dutch (who used to run these undertakings efficiently) left the country. But from this point on, Sukarno had only one sanction left—that of force.

★   ★   ★

In the West Irian (Dutch New Guinea) campaign, Sukarno had a bear by the tail and he was never able to let go. In the end he won.

There is little point now in analysing in detail the rights and wrongs of the Indonesian claim to West Irian. When Holland and Indonesia agreed at the end of 1949 on terms for the transfer of sovereignty over the islands of the archipelago, the future of West Irian was deliberately left unsettled, the agreement providing only that the question should be 'determined through negotiations' within a year. The first discussions took place in December, 1950, and the talks broke down. We shall never know now what would have been the result if the case had been tested before the International Court. Some lawyers have suggested that Indonesia's legal case was much better than has often been assumed; but of course the dispute went deeper than law.

Many people have been puzzled by the lengths to which both Sukarno and the Dutch were prepared to go in order to control a territory so essentially unrewarding as the western half of New Guinea. It can be said at once that neither expected to derive any economic benefit from it. The country cost the Dutch a great deal of money. However true Canning's statement that

> *'In matters of commerce the fault of the Dutch*
> *Is giving too little and asking too much'*

might seem to be in respect of their years of empire over the islands of Indonesia, the territory of West Irian contained little hope of profit.

Each side had other, and different, reasons. The Indonesian nationalists laid claim from the beginning to the entire territory of the Netherlands East Indies, which included Dutch New Guinea; for reasons of prestige it was subsequently difficult for President Sukarno to relinquish the claim. There may also have been a contributory wish to gain a strategic foothold close to Australia and open to the Pacific. Much more important was the strong desire, based on hatred and deep suspicion of the Dutch, to remove them completely and finally from the area; many Indonesian leaders believed that the Dutch were implacably hostile to the new Republic and that they would always be hoping to extend their influence, especially in the Moluccas.

The Dutch were in large measure, though not entirely, actuated by considerations of prestige. They had historically always been a colonial power, and after the humiliation of the war and the struggle against the Indonesian nationalists they were anxious to retain at least some remnants of their history; moreover, they were sufficiently hostile to the Indonesian nationalists not to be averse to withholding from them anything which they had the power—and a reasonable excuse— to retain. The excuse was in any case a good one, namely that the Papuans of New Guinea are not Indonesians by race or history, and that when the time came for them to determine their own future they ought to be given the chance to choose independence or union with their Papuan neighbours in Australian New Guinea. Finally the Dutch, resentful as they had always been of the lack of support they received after the war from the Labour Government of Australia, were nevertheless no doubt later influenced by the extreme unwillingness of the subsequent Menzies Government to welcome a potentially communist Indonesia on to Australia's doorstep in New Guinea.

Later still, Australian opinion changed again, when the threat of communism in Indonesia appeared to be held in check by the Army, and when it began to become apparent that in modern strategic terms Indonesia was not likely to be any more dangerous at a distance of 175 miles from Cape York than she was already with Timor only 250 miles from

Cape Talbot. This impression was greatly strengthened by a visit paid to Australia in 1961 by the reassuringly moderate General Nasution.

There can be no doubt that to the mass of Indonesians the future of West Irian was a matter of more or less complete indifference until the end of the 1950s, if not to this day. For years it remained no more than a subject for passionate speeches by demagogues. By an ironical coincidence, the ceremonial creation in February, 1958, of a 'National Front for the Liberation of West Irian' was immediately followed by the outbreak of the rebellions in Sumatra and Sulawesi which for years effectually prevented Indonesia from even contemplating military action in support of her claim.

It was not, in fact, until the autumn of 1961 that the surrender of the rebels made this possible; and by that time West Irian had become for Sukarno both a major obsession and his sole means of uniting patriotic feeling. His speeches, designed as much as anything to divert attention from the economic problems of the country, became more and more bellicose. The economic problems had become, by the end of 1961, acute; inflation was increasing, and there was a serious food shortage in Java, forcing the government to import rice from abroad. Only by working up public feeling about West Irian was Sukarno able to pose once more as the 'Great Leader of the Revolution', which splendid title the Madjelis had conferred on him in 1960.

Moreover, there were armed forces available to apply pressure on the Dutch. How good they were—and are—is anyone's guess. The Army at least was fairly well equipped; the Air Force was beginning to be; the Navy was at that time short of ships. Arrangements had been made in January to buy some £130 million worth of arms from Russia, and some had already been secured from the West. General Nasution had succeeded during the rebellion in organising an efficiently executed combined operation and landing, but it had met with no effective resistance. At no stage in the rebellion had the real fighting quality of the troops been thoroughly tested.

It was a quite new Army, without any longer traditions than could be accumulated in sporadic fighting against the Dutch and in limited campaigns against the various rebels; but its officers were young and enthusiastic, willing to accept heavy responsibilities and with a strong *esprit de corps*.

Preparations for possible operations against the Dutch in West Irian began to be made in the second half of 1961. It became obvious that the Dutch would not reach any voluntary agreement that did not safeguard the rights of the Papuans to self-determination; they offered to transfer the territory to the control of the United Nations, but this Sukarno refused to consider. Towards the end of the year, Sukarno announced that on December 19 he would 'issue his commands' to the armed forces for the 'liberation' of West Irian. Probably he intended to do no more than make a belligerent speech, in the hope that the Dutch would take fright; but as things turned out his hand was forced by the Indian invasion of Goa two days before his speech was due to be made. Unwilling to be outdone in anti-colonial bravado, Sukarno took the plunge and announced that West Irian would be 'liberated' by force. Troops were collected in Sulawesi, whither Sukarno went in state in January, 1962, to encourage them. It was his first visit to this important island since 1957, despite the rebellions and other troubles it had suffered, and someone threw a bomb at him there (without effect).

It is doubtful whether General Nasution—or even Sukarno—ever contemplated a successful operation to take the whole of West Irian by force. What was probably planned was an invasion to occupy a beachhead: once the flag had been planted on Irian the immediate claims of honour would have been satisfied, and an interminable wrangle would have developed in the United Nations until perhaps the Dutch would have tired of the whole business. In the event it did not come to that, so that we shall never know whether the plan would have been successful. There were various attempts at infiltration by small sea landings and minor parachute operations, none of which was particularly effective. Talks with the Dutch and various intermediaries broke down in March, and parachute operations were stepped up in June. In July, lacking any stronger support from their allies, the Dutch decided to accept a compromise arrangement for handing over the territory.

Agreement was reached on August 15, and on October 1, 1962, West Irian was handed over to the temporary control of a United Nations administrator. A United Nations Technical Authority was to run the territory until May 1, 1963, when the administration was to be taken over by Indonesia. Indonesia had to accept arrangements for self-determination by the inhabitants by 1969, the Papuans being given then the chance to decide, under United Nations auspices, whether to remain part of Indonesia or look elsewhere. Sukarno had always in the past refused to commit himself to this, but no doubt he felt unable to let slip the chance to enjoy a temporary triumph—which time might well confirm, if everything went (or was made to go) well.

* * *

The great crusade was over. There were victory celebrations and many speeches. Unfortunately Indonesia's fundamental —and increasingly serious—problems were no nearer solution. So far from West Irian being an economic asset, it was bound to cost Indonesia a lot of money if her development of it was not to compare unfavourably with that of the Dutch, who had been running the territory at a net loss of about £13 million a year.

Meanwhile Indonesia's gold reserves were exhausted, her formerly favourable trade balance was disastrously in debit, and her military expenditure was far heavier than her economy could possibly afford. A country richer in resources than almost any in Asia was on the verge of bankruptcy, and the government continued to talk in terms of grandiose long-term development plans instead of tackling the immediate problems with drastic and effective measures.

It seemed as if Sukarno was unable to focus his undoubted

ability on the details of these problems. The chronic tendency to seek an external counter-irritant began to show itself again. There were vague references to Portuguese Timor and 'colonialism'. More dangerous was the support given to the Brunei rebellion and the growing hostility to plans for the Malaysian Federation, culminating in naked aggression and totalitarian measures against British firms in Indonesia. In September, 1963, a government-organised mob burned down the British embassy in Djakarta.

Meanwhile 'Guided Democracy' continued virtually to function through the Army. Sukarno was in theory a national dictator, and his presence in Djakarta held the two forces of the Army and the communist PKI in balance at the centre. The exact strength of the PKI has always been in dispute. At the last elections to be held it polled 8 million votes, and its party membership has been stated to be as high as 3 million, with millions more supporters in the communist-led unions. For official registration purposes, the party leadership gave 600,000 as the party figure in 1961, but the best informed estimates suggested a true membership of around 1,500,000 then. It was certainly higher in 1965.

D. N. Aidit, the PKI leader, played his cards with skill and loyally supported Sukarno, who in return preserved the communists from the more drastic measures which General Nasution would have liked to take against them. In 1962 he admitted them to his Cabinet. Thus Sukarno was a genuine balancing force between the two great rivals for power. The PKI was not strong enough to gain power by a *coup d'état* so long as the Army remained at its inflated strength: how long Indonesia could afford to maintain that strength is another matter, and the PKI might well have felt that it could bide its time so long as Sukarno was there and on its side.

Perhaps it did feel this. The causes and even the direction of the attempted *coup* on the night of September 30, 1965, are, at the time of writing, still obscure. Certainly the Army was becoming alarmed at the possibility that Sukarno might yield to communist pleas for the arming of 'workers and peasants' in a kind of militia that would have given the PKI much greater relative strength. An Army *coup* may have been imminent. Or the PKI, advised by Peking, may have miscalculated its moment. At all events, a section of the presidential guard, led by a Colonel Untung, attempted a *coup* in Djakarta, with support from communist sympathisers in the Air Force high command. There was also a rising in central Java. The *coup* failed, as did an attempt on General Nasution's life. The communists were sufficiently implicated to enable the Army to suppress them, and PKI leaders went underground.

At present, outside Djakarta, the Army still virtually rules the country. In the autonomous regions which comprise the most important areas of the country, military governors and army commanders are still responsible for rehabilitating the districts recovering from rebellions, for local administration and agricultural development. Moreover, their rule is for the most part beneficent and efficient. If only there were a competent central government in Djakarta with a coherent economic policy, the recovery of this potentially wealthy country would be possible. But it would involve the slashing of the impossibly onerous defence budget, the calling off of 'confrontation' and other foreign adventures, and the encouragement of foreign investment.

Without stability at home and in external relations, even the essential foreign aid cannot be secured—although a rapprochement with the Dutch since the West Irian settlement has helped a little, and China is ready to secure influence through aid.

Meanwhile, in the chaos of Djakarta or the peace of Bogor, Sukarno went on dreaming of empire and leadership of the 'new emerging forces' of the world. Visions of the former glories of Madjapahit, perhaps stretching as far as Malaya and the Philippines, are always with him. He is, in fact, the perfect type of the self-righteous but unscrupulous imperialist that he denounces in his speeches.

As this book goes to press, the future of the 65-year-old Sukarno is completely uncertain. It is still possible that a complete economic breakdown might provoke the Army to get rid of him; but, despite negligible foreign exchange reserves, the loss of trade with Singapore, rampant inflation and near-starvation in parts of Java, Indonesia has hitherto somehow avoided complete breakdown.

In February, 1966, Sukarno appeared to have recovered some ground, and even dismissed General Nasution. But in March there were violent student riots in Djakarta, and Sukarno's position looked dangerous.

The new Army Commander-in-Chief, General Suharto, has emerged as a strong man pledged to put things right. Whether he can succeed, and what will now be the position of General Nasution, is still doubtful. But whatever happens, Indonesia cannot long afford to be without competent government in Djakarta; history suggests that the time may be approaching for another round of separatist rebellions outside Java.

8

The Asian Dilemma

So we come to the end of this largely historical survey of the countries and problems of South Asia. It will be apparent that the forces which we saw in 1945 striving against one another to fill the vacuum left by Japan's defeat and the withdrawal of colonial powers have neither worked themselves out nor achieved a satisfactory equilibrium.

Both neutralist 'non-alignment' and collective security seem largely to have failed as effective policies. SEATO is more or less a dead letter. Of the great neutralist leaders who dreamed of a 'third force' in Asia, Nehru is dead and his country at loggerheads with Pakistan and menaced by Chinese aggression; U Nu is a prisoner, and Burma under a military dictatorship increasingly subservient to communist China; Sukarno has turned to aggressive imperialism, and is prepared to align himself with China if his expansionist designs are thereby helped; Prince Sihanouk almost despairs of his country's neutrality, and believes that China must ultimately become dominant in South-east Asia.

At the time of writing, while Britain strains her military and economic resources to defend a disintegrating Malaysia against Sukarno's aggression, the military and economic strength of the United States forms the only barrier to communist expansion in Indo-China and perhaps beyond.

Communism, although permitted by Sukarno's recent incompetence to come within sight of success in Indonesia, has failed everywhere in South Asia to win power or supreme influence by peaceful means. This is a lesson of the utmost importance, and one which it appears Western left-wingers will never learn.

The arguments used are invariably circular and self-contradictory. We are told that communism gains ground because of poverty and starvation and that democracy must meet it with economic aid and in a 'battle for the minds of men'. When communist insurgency threatens the independence of Laos or South Vietnam, we are told that it is futile to oppose it by force of arms.

The fact is that, despite poverty and propaganda, communism has not been successful anywhere except by force of arms. Moreover, Laos and South Vietnam are much less free and much nearer starvation than they were before communism 'liberated' large parts of those countries. In short, what we are being invited by so-called 'liberal opinion' to do is to acquiesce in the conquest of peaceful countries by alien forces.

Nor has there yet been the slightest indication that Ho Chi Minh (or Sukarno, for that matter) has any intention of settling for a peaceful compromise when he thinks he can secure all his aims by force. And the people who now urge us to 'negotiate' with the aggressors are the very ones who before the war inveighed against the 'appeasement' of the European dictators. It appears that aggression is not aggression, nor the sacrifice of helpless peoples appeasement, when the dictators involved are of the left.

This is not, of course, to say that political solutions to the problems of Laos, Vietnam and Indonesian-Malayan relations are not essential, or that negotiations to that end should not be entered upon whenever there is the slightest chance of fruitful parley. But it is mere fatuous folly (or worse) to scream for negotiations with aggressors who will not compromise, while seeking to sabotage the only measures that can restrain the aggressors' use of force.

The aggressors may yet be willing to compromise—but only if they have been met with sufficient force to convince them that they cannot win by force.

Can Vietnam be neutralised, as General de Gaulle and others have suggested? Not while Ho Chi Minh thinks he can conquer South Vietnam. He will never make the first move to neutralise himself. Should the United States and

Britain, then, yield to the popular clamour to avert an escalating war in which 'our boys' may be called upon to die in a cause imperfectly understood and already half lost? But this hideous choice is one perfectly familiar from past history. Are the answers likely to be any different now?

Alternatively, should we believe the experts on China, who assure us that China is not *au fond* 'expansionist', but seeks only to look after her overseas nationals and to re-establish her suzerainty over areas traditionally in her sphere of influence? Two answers suggest themselves. The first is that it would indeed be very nice if China's territorial ambitions were strictly limited; but if the West and the neutralists relied on this and then found they were wrong, it would by then be too late to rescue the immolated victims. The second is that the argument of 'suzerainty' and 'spheres of influence' is a purely imperialist one, with no more validity in the case of China than it had in the early days of the colonialist powers. It is in any case an argument that would justify the Cambodians in trying to conquer Laos and much of Thailand, or indeed Britain in invading France.

There is every argument for trying to bring China back into the comity of nations, undoing some of the follies of American policy towards her after 1949. But, so long as China remains aloof, it would be wise to be prepared for trouble while seeking earnestly to avert it.

*　　*　　*

Almost as dangerous as left-wing efforts to appease or abet communist aggression in Asia is the recent right-wing revival of efforts to cut aid to the uncommitted countries of Asia. It is natural that there should still be smouldering embers of resentment against the countries which threw off the colonialist yoke and then refused to join the Western alliance. But the sooner the embers are stamped out the better for the world.

It is even more natural that there should be resentment against countries which have shown themselves 'ungrateful' for aid, and disappointment with those that have 'wasted' aid and degenerated into economic or administrative chaos. But if aid is given with the object of earning gratitude, it is wasted from the start. Moreover, the lack of competence in Burma, Ceylon or Indonesia must be blamed as much on the former colonial powers as on the nationalist leaders. We were ready enough to blame the Belgians for what happened in the Congo.

Indeed, the miracle is that so much has been achieved, and that government has been so well carried on in so many countries. Whatever the future may hold for them, India and Malaya have earned respect and trust. Nor is it remarkable that the harvest of Western democracy should fail at the first sowing of the seeds. It took long enough for the Western world to evolve it and make it work. And it may well be that in India and Pakistan, in Malaya and Thailand, in Ceylon and even perhaps in Indonesia, there will mature political systems that will be democratic and viable.

Just as Asia must in the end find its own answers to its own problems, so the West must solve its own Asian dilemma for itself. The errors of the Dulles era are things of the past. Alignment may yet come, but it cannot be forced by the West. Probably only China could provoke it—one way or the other. Neutralism may yet prevail—although its prospects are not too bright—and we could do with more of it in Indo-China. The West has much to offer Asia, and much still to learn. Patience and good will are essential.

It may be that in the end the only formula for the containment of China is the complete neutralisation of all South Asia, from Afghanistan to Indonesia, under a joint Western and Soviet guarantee followed by planned economic aid jointly provided by East and West. It will take a long time for Russia and America to reach agreement on this. In the meantime, aggressors who will not negotiate must be resisted by force of arms.